THE REAL
HORNBLOWER

OTHER BOOKS BY BRYAN PERRETT

THE REAL HORNBLOWER

The Life & Times of
ADMIRAL SIR JAMES GORDON GCB

BRYAN PERRETT

Pen & Sword
MARITIME

First published in Great Britain in 1997 by
Arms and Armour Press, an imprint of the Cassell Group
Wellington House, 125 Strand, London WC2R 0RB
Re-printed in paperback format in 1998, 1999, and 2000 by
Arms and Armour Press

Re-printed in 1998 in paperback format by
Naval Institute Press, Annapolis, USA

Reprinted in this format in 2013 by
PEN & SWORD MARITIME
An imprint of
Pen & Sword Books Ltd
47 Church Street
Barnsley, South Yorkshire
S70 2AS

ISBN 978 1 78159 195 6

Printed and bound in England
By CPI Group (UK) Ltd, Croydon, CR0 4YY

Pen & Sword Books Ltd incorporates the Imprints of Pen & Sword Aviation,
Pen & Sword Family History, Pen & Sword Maritime, Pen & Sword Military,
Pen & Sword Discovery, Pen & Sword Politics, Pen & Sword Archaeology,
Pen & Sword Atlas, Wharncliffe Local History, Wharncliffe True Crime,
Wharncliffe Transport, Pen & Sword Select, Pen & Sword Military Classics,
Leo Cooper, The Praetorian Press, Claymore Press, Remember When,
Seaforth Publishing and Frontline Publishing

For a complete list of Pen & Sword titles please contact
PEN & SWORD BOOKS LIMITED
47 Church Street, Barnsley, South Yorkshire, S70 2AS, England
E-mail: enquiries@pen-and-sword.co.uk
Website: www.pen-and-sword.co.uk

CONTENTS

ACKNOWLEDGEMENTS

I should like to express my sincere appreciation and thanks to the following for their kind advice, assistance and encouragement: to Michael Wilson, who, while serving with the Naval Historical Branch, considerately provided source material which, when followed through, suggested that there was indeed a case to answer; to Rachel Mackenzie of the Maritime Information Centre, National Maritime Museum, who always dealt with my numerous requests for photo copies, chart details, warship histories and other matters with good humoured efficiency; to Christopher Gray, Head of the Picture Research Information Division, National Maritime Museum, who produced so many interesting illustrations of Admiral Gordon's life; to John Montgomery, Librarian, Royal United Services Institute for Defence Studies; to John J. Slonaker, Chief, Historical Reference Branch, US Army Military History Institute, Carlisle, Pennsylvania; Bernard F. Cavalcante, Head, Operational Archives Branch, Naval Historical Center, Washington, DC; Vincent J. Vaise, Fort McHenry National Monument; John M. Dervan, Historian, Fort Belvoir, Virginia; The Maryland Historical Society; and Alice S. Creighton, Head, Special Collections and Archives, Nimitz Library, US Naval Academy, Annapolis, Maryland, for their invaluable advice regarding the Potomac and Baltimore operations of 1814; and finally to various departments of Aberdeen City Council and Aberdeenshire County Council for producing so much interesting background material on the Admiral's family.

Bryan Perrett
May 1997

Introduction
A HERO DEEP IN SHADOW

Horatio Hornblower, as the admirable Mr Florence MacCarthy Knox might have commented to his close friend the Irish RM, was born in the middle of his life and from that point proceeded both forwards and backwards in time; further, it might be added, he was conceived long after his death, a circumstance which could be described as the making of him.

Hornblower was, in fact, conceived aboard a tramp steamer named the *Margaret Johnson* in which his creator, C. S. Forester, had taken passage from California to England via a number of Central American ports and the Panama Canal. During the early part of the voyage it seems that the Anglo–American War of 1812 was in Forester's thoughts, and in particular the definition as contained within the December 1814 Treaty of Ghent as to when hostilities should legally be deemed to have ended. This was a most important consideration at a time when the speed of communications, whether written or verbal, was no faster than the ships in which they were conveyed. In their wisdom the peacemakers decreed that in the North Atlantic the war would end twelve days after the ratification of the Treaty; in the Baltic, the statutory period was forty days; and in the remoter reaches of the Pacific, one hundred and twenty days. The fact that the last naval engagement of the war – the capture of HMS *Penguin* by the USS *Hornet* off Tristan da Cunha – took place fully five weeks after Congress had ratified the Treaty emphasised the very remoteness of commanders from their political masters.

As the *Margaret Johnson* meandered from one steamy and romantically derelict harbour to another, Forester reflected that the whole of the Central American isthmus and the entire western seaboard of South America had once formed part of Spain's colonial empire. During the Napoleonic Wars that empire had begun to break up as the inhabitants of successive provinces and vice-royalties fought for and won their independence from the mother country; further, the political pattern was even more confused by Spain's having been first an ally of Napoleon, and then his bitter enemy.

A plot began to form in Forester's mind. Suppose, for example, that in 1808 the Admiralty dispatched a frigate around Cape Horn with the purpose of

7

supporting a specific group of colonial *insurrectos* on the west coast of Central America. Having seized the major Spanish naval unit in the area by *coup de main*, the frigate's captain hands her over to the revolutionaries who are led by an unstable local tyrant. Shortly afterwards, Spanish loyalists tell him that Spain and Great Britain, recently foes, are now allied in the common cause against Napoleon, knowledge which his long isolation from Europe has denied him. Horrified by the discovery that he has apparently been fighting on the wrong side, he decides that he must either re-take the other vessel and restore her to the Spanish Navy, or destroy her; nothing less will suffice if he is to escape professional disgrace. The climax of the story is a hard-fought and protracted duel between the two ships from which the British frigate emerges the winner.

If the geo-political setting was original, the story was not and would be recognised by fiction writers as a standard formula in which a tragic mistake is redeemed under the most difficult circumstances. For the project to succeed two further elements would have to be present. The first was strong characterisation, particularly in the case of the frigate's captain, who was to be named Horatio Hornblower. Forester, already an established and successful novelist, was clearly a perceptive observer of behaviour under stress, but could he penetrate the thought patterns of a Royal Naval officer of 1808? In fact few men were better qualified for such a task, for in 1927 he had purchased three volumes of the *Naval Chronicle*, a monthly magazine written by naval officers for naval officers, published between the years 1790 and 1820. 'Those volumes', wrote Forester, 'were read and re-read during the months that followed, and perhaps I absorbed some of the atmosphere; certainly I became very familiar with the special mental attitude of naval officers at that time regarding various aspects of their profession.'

Thus he discovered the type of captain he was seeking, but there was another influence at work, too. Forester had a fondness in his heroes for what he chose to call the Man Alone, the individual who depends solely on his own resources and reserves to solve his problems, and who can expect little or no assistance from other quarters. By and large, the Man Alone was an apparently unremarkable person whom Fate had placed in jeopardy but who could, with courage and imagination, influence events beyond his normal sphere. Here was a hero with whom the average reader would willingly identify, hoping and believing that in similar circumstances he would act likewise.

The character of Horatio Hornblower steadily emerged while the *Margaret Johnson* passed through the Panama Canal and left the blue waters of the Caribbean for the grey wastes of the North Atlantic. Unlike that of most heroes of popular historical fiction, it contained a startling number of negative qualities. Hornblower was lonely with a loneliness that exceeded that of command; he was somewhat introverted, sensitive and sharply self-critical; he was reserved and not notably gifted with a sense of humour; he survived solely on his pay yet was forced to maintain appearances appropriate to his rank; he suffered agonies of sea-sickness at the beginning of every voyage; his performance with sword and pistol were average for a profession of arms, but his horsemanship was a joke; he was diffident in his dealings with the opposite sex, to whom he generally left the initiative, and for that reason had slid into an unfortunate marriage; he was painfully conscious of his gangling appearance and awkward movements; and he was tone deaf.

On the other hand, his long years of experience had produced in him a very competent professional, skilled in seamanship and the varied aspects of naval gunnery and tactics. He ran a very tight ship but was averse to flogging. With the lower deck he was firm and distant but fair and above all consistent, and he led from the front in moments of danger. He did not expect the men to like him and whenever they revealed that they did he was acutely embarrassed. He took pleasure in mathematics and was therefore an excellent navigator. Indeed, it was these same logical thought processes that enabled him to think through his tactical problems to their conclusion. Gifted with too much imagination, he knew paralysing fear yet managed to suppress it, so demonstrating the true essence of courage.

In short, therefore, Horatio Hornblower was not the swashbuckling sea-dog familiar to earlier generations of readers. On the contrary, he was a recognisable naval officer with human strengths, weaknesses, feelings, fears and hopes and this in itself would appeal to a public accustomed to heroes whose natural superiority enabled them to achieve their objectives without apparent difficulty.

There remained the second element in the book's construction, that relating to the technical aspects of the story. Here there was no cause for concern, for Forester was steeped in the literature of the Napoleonic Wars and was fully conversant with the tactics and weapon systems of contemporary land and sea warfare. His research was thorough and meticulous, his knowledge of standing and running rigging exact, his details of ship management realistic and the orders given by his officers entirely appropriate to the circumstances. The detail into which he went was quite remarkable and contributed in no small measure to the success of his work. Far from boring the reader, that same detail was used to raise the tension to an almost unbearable level, and whether the work involved was splicing a vital rope or replacing the blown vent-piece of a cannon, it was generally carried out in desperate circumstances with time a critical factor.

In due course, *Margaret Johnson* docked in England and Forester began his book. It was published in the United Kingdom as *The Happy Return* and in the United States as *Beat to Quarters*. It was instantly successful and the public's interest in Hornblower was stimulated to such an extent that it wanted to know a great deal more about him. Forester obliged his readers with two related novels, *A Ship of the Line* and *Flying Colours*, covering the years 1810 and 1811. These found Hornblower engaged off the north-east coast of Spain, losing his ship in heroic circumstances, suffering capture and incarceration at the hands of the French, contriving his escape and ultimately seizing a vessel in which to return to the United Kingdom.

At this point the Second World War intervened in Forester's career. He entered the Ministry of Information and sailed with the Royal Navy to collect material for his book *The Ship*. He then moved to the United States, where he used his pen to fight the battles of his native land in the country of his adoption.

It was six years before he returned to his hero. By now he was suffering from arteriosclerosis, the progressive effects of which were measurable and pronounced terminal. Against medical advice he wrote *The Commodore*, which took Hornblower to the Baltic in the momentous year of 1812. To my mind this book is the best of the Hornblower series and there is good reason to believe that Forester thought so too.

Sometimes, courage does bring its own unexpected reward. For no identifiable medical reason, the progress of the horrible disease was suddenly suspended. Forester would always be an invalid but he was alive. *The Commodore* had been another remarkable success and, perhaps with a sense of gratitude, he decided to use the remission to complete the story of Horatio Hornblower's service career. A series of books followed, which I have listed by biographical and date order rather than the order of their publication. They were: *Mr Midshipman Hornblower* (1794–7); *Lieutenant Hornblower* (1800); *Hornblower and the* Hotspur (1803–5); *Hornblower and the Crisis* (1805); *Hornblower and the* Atropos (1805–8); *Lord Hornblower* (1813–14); and *Hornblower in the West Indies* (1821–3). The cycle was complete and Hornblower, after Nelson the most famous naval officer of his generation, lives on as one of literature's best-loved characters.

However, like any author required to produce a series of absorbing, unusual yet entirely credible plots, Forester discovered that the fount of inspiration was a fickle thing that flowed freely when it was least required and not at all when it was desperately needed. There is, as he comments in *The Hornblower Companion*, no more futile exercise than sitting down to think of a plot. Plots cannot be summoned; they appear in their own time and in the place of their choosing, and if they are not jotted down at once they will probably escape forever. But what if one's publisher demands a plot, quickly and without argument? The only recourse is to real life and accumulated experience which enables one to choose a situation and develop a story around it. This, Forester frankly admits, is how many of Hornblower's adventures were conceived. He also admits to meddling, in a harmless sort of way, with the facts of history. The Duke of Wellington, for example, did not have a sister named Barbara, and the duc d'Angoulême's presence in Le Havre gives rise to some surprise since on the date in question he is known to have been in Bordeaux, several hundred miles away. In such cases, Forester comments wryly, 'The student is faced with a choice between history and Hornblower!'

The essential character of Hornblower, of course, remains Forester's own creation and since the best writing projects the personality of its author we can see in Hornblower strands of Forester's own modesty and quiet brand of high courage. Nevertheless it was interesting to speculate as to which of Hornblower's adventures were based on real events, and whether these involved the same officer or were simply samples from a selection of distinguished careers. To me the latter always seemed the more probable until, quite by chance, I began to accumulate evidence to the contrary.

Of course, the setting of *The Happy Return* existed solely in the confines of the author's plot, for in 1808 the Royal Navy was stretched to the limit by its commitments in the Atlantic, the Baltic, the Mediterranean and along the trade routes to India and the East Indies, without having to detach a precious frigate on a mission of questionable value to the west coast of South and Central America; the fact was, the Navy had better fish to fry than could ever be found in those waters.

Yet it was there, more than ten years later and with the Napoleonic Wars beginning to fade into history, that one of England's most distinguished seamen added yet further laurels to an already remarkable career. His name was Thomas Cochrane and there are sufficient points of similarity between his story and Hornblower's for a degree of comparison to be made. His record reads like a series of desperate fictional episodes and provided much inspiration for one of his junior officers, the future Captain Marryat, the author of *Mr Midshipman Easy* and other adventure stories.

In 1818 Cochrane's career entered troubled waters. His name was linked with a Stock Exchange scandal, in consequence of which he was imprisoned for a brief period and dismissed the service. He was not long finding employment, for in the Americas the Spanish colonies were in full revolt against their mother country, and the revolutionary government of Chile offered him command of its small but growing Navy. He travelled out immediately with his wife and family, arriving in Valparaiso in November, and the following month hoisted his flag in the 50-gun *O'Higgins*, named after General Bernardo O'Higgins, the Supreme Director of the Chilean Government.

The title was not lost on Forester, for the deranged leader of the rebels in *The Happy Return* was also named El Supremo, although clearly no derogatory comparison with O'Higgins was intended. Nor was the size of Cochrane's flagship, which the Chileans had captured from the Spaniards, under whom she had served as the *Maria Isabel*. In the Royal Navy, 50-gun ships were classed as Fourth Rates. In time of war they fell awkwardly between two stools, for while they were too small to take their place in the line of battle, they lacked the sailing qualities of the less powerful frigates. The virtues of the Fifties lay in that they were cheap to build and maintain and that, being two-deckers, they could provide accommodation for an admiral and his staff. In peacetime the major maritime powers employed their Fifties as flagships on foreign stations. All the same, it would have been most unwise for a frigate such as *Lydia* (36), in which Hornblower entered the Pacific, to engage from choice in a gunnery contest with the *Natividad* (50) of *The Happy Return*. The imbalance was great but Forester knew that it could be overcome by better seamanship, gunnery, damage control and discipline aboard the smaller vessel. Thus, when *Lydia* and *Natividad* met for the last time and fought their epic duel, it was the former, badly battered, which survived, while her opponent went to the bottom.

Cochrane virtually swept the Spaniards off the sea. In June 1820 he captured Valdivia, the enemy's last remaining naval base in Chile, and he then moved north to blockade Callao in Peru. Here, on 5 November, he led a spectacular cutting-out expedition which captured the frigate *Esmeralda* (44) and would have taken other vessels in the Spanish squadron as well if one of his subordinates had not departed from the pre-arranged plan. The method employed was reminiscent of Hornblower's initial capture of the *Natividad*.

Superficially, the frequent presence of Lady Cochrane aboard her husband's flagship can be seen to have given Forester a convenient excuse for inserting Lady Barbara Wellesley aboard Hornblower's *Lydia*, thereby providing the romantic interest that had hitherto been lacking in the novel's plot. But the problem was that Lady Cochrane was the archetypal heroine, as beautiful as she was brave; on one occasion, for example, when the Chileans deserted their posts under the fire of a coastal battery's red-hot shot, she assisted the one-armed Cochrane load and fire *O'Higgins'* guns himself until the shamefaced seamen returned to their weapons. Such a woman would have completely dominated the gentle Hornblower and destroyed his fragile self-confidence. With great skill, however, Forester paints a very different picture of Lady Barbara, whose long Wellesley nose prevents her being described as a great beauty, and whose quieter but firm and sometimes haughty nature complements rather than obliterates the Captain. With *Lydia* engaged in her death-grapple with *Natividad*, Lady Barbara is not to be found on the gundeck, but below in the screaming semi-darkness, giving what help she can as the surgeon's knife and saw do their bloody work.

Even today, Lord Cochrane is still regarded as a national hero in Chile and Peru. When his work there was finished he had an equally dramatic career as commander of, first, the Navy of Brazil, and then that of Greece. In 1831 he inherited the earldom of Dundonald and the following year was reinstated in the Royal Navy, with flag rank.

And yet, despite the startling number of coincidences relating to their operations in the Pacific, Cochrane could never have served as the model for Hornblower. He was always of the Establishment, whatever his rank, whereas Hornblower, for much of his service, remained entirely without influence. Moreover, as a contemporary observer was to comment, Cochrane was 'wilful, original, rash of temper, incontinent of speech, with a genius not only for quarrelling with his superiors, but for proving himself right and them wrong'. Originality of thought apart, these are not the qualities with which Forester endowed his hero.

With regard to *A Ship of the Line*, and indeed every subsequent book in the series, the names of Lord James de Saumarez and Sir Edward Pellew, later Lord Exmouth, have been suggested as those of Hornblower's prototype. De Saumarez belonged to an old Guernsey family and, like Hornblower in *The Commodore*, at one period held a command under trying circumstances in the Baltic. This is far from being the only echo of de Saumarez in Hornblower's exploits, but one must remember that he was much older than Hornblower – he was actually a little older than Nelson – and a great deal more senior. Much the same might be said of Pellew, who made his name as a brilliant frigate captain, but in his case Forester emphasises that he is not our man by making the fictional Midshipman Hornblower serve under him, in *Arethusa* and then in *Indefatigable*, thereby ensuring that he had regular contact with the enemy and ample opportunity to display his initiative.

A far more serious objection to this suggestion is the fact that both de Saumarez and Pellew were men of quite exceptional ability, and this in itself confirms that neither of them could have served as the model for Hornblower. The whole point about Hornblower was that he was a capable but average naval officer of the period, lacking position, influence and money, and was in no way exceptional; had it been otherwise, the character would have lost much impact and appeal. Nevertheless, after a long and eventful career, Hornblower was not only honoured by his countrymen but had reached the top of his profession, entirely by his own efforts and sheer determination. The question now facing the curious is whether such a modest hero could be found among the shadows cast by his more extrovert contemporaries.

Quite by chance I discovered the answer when researching the Chesapeake Bay Campaign of 1814, an interesting campaign that witnessed both the burning of Washington's public buildings and the writing of the American National Anthem during the British bombardment of Baltimore. While Major-General Robert Ross' small army of Peninsular War veterans was marching on Washington from its landing place on the River Patuxent, the Royal Navy had sent a diversionary force, consisting of two frigates, three bomb ketches and a rocket vessel, up the treacherous Potomac to the town of Alexandria, a few miles downstream from the American capital. Despite severe navigational problems, prepared defences and every obstacle which the Americans could place in its path, the little squadron reached its objective, captured the town, and retired down-river in the teeth of even greater opposition, bringing 21 prize vessels with it, for comparatively trivial loss.

Of the squadron's commander, named by Forester in his *Naval War of 1812* simply as 'Captain Gordon, RN', I knew nothing, but the 1849 edition of *The Naval Biographical Dictionary*, published while the officer in question was still living, provided a number of very interesting answers. James Alexander Gordon, it seemed, had enjoyed a very long and active career and had seen more than his share of battle and sudden death. The Potomac venture apart, there had been fights against odds, hard-fought single-ship actions, cutting-out expeditions and landings on enemy coasts. His achievements were recorded regularly in *The London Gazette*, and in 1813 the *Naval Chronicle* contained an article devoted exclusively to his career to date. Clearly he was a courageous, determined and resourceful commander. He was also evidently something of a sentimentalist, for after the Napoleonic Wars he returned to the same frigate, HMS *Active*, which he had commanded during the most spectacular years of his career. Apparently he got on extremely well with the lower deck, for in due course he was appointed Lieutenant-Governor then Governor of the Royal Naval Hospital at Greenwich, the naval equivalent of the Royal Hospital, Chelsea. His name would certainly be well known throughout the Navy and, during the war years, to the general public as well.

With a growing sense of *deja vu* I realised that I was already familiar with several episodes in Gordon's career and that such familiarity could only have stemmed from the Hornblower cycle. This I might have dismissed as simple coincidence had it not been for a quite uncharacteristic break in Forester's usually meticulous style. In *The Naval War of 1812* he devotes very little space indeed to the Potomac expedition, although it was one of the most remarkable episodes of the entire war. What he does say is based on Gordon's personal entry in *The Naval Biographical Dictionary*, yet, as we have seen, he refers solely to 'Captain Gordon, RN' as being its commander. This in itself is strange, for when referring to other officers of note, British or American, he gives their full names, family backgrounds and details of their service careers; and Gordon's *curriculum vitae* lay before him as he wrote. Further, there were numerous Gordons to be found in the contemporary *Naval List*, and many of them were serving in America, including at least one with the same Christian names. The great majority of readers would not bother to look further; those that did would require the trained eye and archival resources of the professional historian. It seemed as though Forester, while compelled to mention Gordon, was deliberately placing obstacles in the path of the inquisitive. But why should he wish to do this, unless he had something important to hide?

An answer was provided by Forester himself. It was one thing for him to write *The Naval War of 1812* as a piece of naval history, but quite another to allow Hornblower to take part in it. American readers would be very angry indeed if Captain Horatio Hornblower were to cross the Atlantic and inflict a defeat on the Navy of whose achievements they were so proud, and British readers would be furious if the reverse were to apply. The answer was, in literary terms, *The Commodore*, which saw Hornblower posted to the Baltic, safely beyond reach of controversy. By coincidence Hornblower's squadron also included bomb ketches and was remarkably similar in composition to that which Gordon took up the Potomac.

It now seemed reasonable to assume that there was indeed a connection in Forester's mind between Gordon and Hornblower, and indeed a partial admission is made by Forester himself in his comments on *The Commodore*, contained in The Hornblower Companion, and written, of course, many years later, when the cycle was complete: 'If Hornblower were not safely employed up the Baltic there was the danger (which I did not like to contemplate) that it would be his bombs that burst in the air over Baltimore!' To say nothing of the fact that it would also be his 'rocket's red glare' that would inspire Mr Francis Scott Key to write the poem universally known today as The Star Spangled Banner!

There was, therefore, a definite connection between Hornblower and Gordon as far as the War of 1812 was concerned. It would, perhaps, be worth establishing whether there were any other points of contact between the two. There were, even at the most superficial level:

- both came from backgrounds that were respectable but not especially affluent;
- both joined the Navy as mere boys in 1793;
- both spent their early service aboard ships of the line and much of their subsequent careers in smaller vessels;
- both, because of their efficiency, rose rapidly in the service, being promoted Lieutenant in 1800, Master and Commander in 1804 and Captain approximately three years later;
- both remained in the much-reduced post-war Navy and obtained sea commands;
- both attained the rank of Admiral of the Fleet.

There were some interesting personal parallels, too. Gordon himself recalls that, in company with the other ship's boys aboard *Arrogant*, he engaged in hunting rats with harpoons; Hornblower, as a newly promoted Midshipman, came across several seamen engaged in a particularly revolting version of this game and, with difficulty, exercised his authority for the first time. The Patriotic Fund presented Hornblower with a gold-hilted sword to commemorate his capture of the Spanish frigate *Castilla*; Gordon's officers presented him with an even more magnificent sword when, seriously wounded, he left the *Active* in 1812, and from the Board of Admiralty he received an inscribed gold medal in recognition of the part he had played in the defeat of a much stronger Franco–Venetian fleet off the island of Lissa. Hornblower received his title on his return from the Baltic; Gordon a knighthood on his return from America. Hornblower retired to the life of a country squire in Kent while Gordon, having received the Freedom of Aberdeen, his native city, was content to end his days among his old seamen at the Royal Hospital, Greenwich. Nor, for reasons which will become clear in due course, do I believe it is simple coincidence that Hornblower's command in *The Happy Return* was named *Lydia*, which also happened to be the name of Gordon's wife.

Such similarities might well be found to exist between the careers of other officers who had joined the Royal Navy in 1793 and survived the Napoleonic Wars, though one might be surprised if such a sequence of coincidences were to repeat itself. I had, therefore, to ponder whether in addition to the striking resemblance between the careers of Gordon and Hornblower, and the established connection between the Potomac/Baltic operations, there were any other incidents by which the two officers could be related. Again, the results of my researches were positive and are set out in the chapters which follow.

It remained only to verify whether, when Forester decided that there would be adequate financial reward in recording Hornblower's entire career, Gordon was present in his thoughts. To extract the maximum possible benefit from his successful formula it was obviously necessary to embrace a service life-span which began with a boy at the start of the wars with Revolutionary France, and ended with an elderly and revered figure of great seniority who had survived into an era in which the Royal Navy's wooden walls were beginning to give way to armour plate, and sails to steam. Quite possibly Forester saw his hero latterly as being one of the last of Nelson's captains, a fact which would confer immense respect and prestige upon him. The last piece in the puzzle was provided by Gordon's obituary in *The Times* of 11 January 1869:

'Sir J. A. Gordon was Admiral of the Fleet and had served in the Royal Navy for the extraordinary period of 75¾ years and was, we believe, the last survivor of Nelson's noble band of Captains.'

In the light of this, Forester's reticence becomes quite intelligible.

There were, it is true, some incidents in Hornblower's story which reflected the achievements of officers other than Gordon, but it is Gordon's life which bears the greatest similarity to Hornblower's and Gordon's career which evidently served as the matrix upon which many of Hornblower's adventures could be laid. Having said that, it is necessary to emphasise that Admiral of the Fleet Sir James Alexander Gordon, GCB, was his own man long before Hornblower was conceived, and therefore commands the respect which he undoubtedly earned.

In recounting his career to the best of my ability, I have, in appropriate circumstances, resorted to footnotes where it and the careers of other officers are apparently reflected in the life of Horatio Hornblower; to have done otherwise might well have resulted in something of a palimpsest.

Chapter 1

THE WILD BOY

U nlike a majority of the Royal Navy's officers, who were drawn from south of a line connecting the Wash with the Severn, James Gordon was a Highlander whose family had been minor gentry in Aberdeenshire for generations.

His grandfather, John Gordon of Beldorny and Wardhouse, was a staunch Jacobite who had been out in the Forty Five and was present in the Young Pretender's army at Culloden. After the battle he managed to escape and reach his own house at Beldorny, situated on the river Deveron some miles from Huntly. When government troops came looking for him, his wife Frances, described as a girl of great spirit and character, hid him under the floorboards of her sitting-room and placed her harpsichord above the trap-door. She gave instructions that the soldiers should be admitted without demur and, while they searched the house from top to bottom, continued to play the instrument. Finding nothing, they departed empty handed. Some months later, the government, whose concern was principally with the more important leaders of the rebellion, wisely decided to display some magnanimity towards lesser participants and granted certain of them, including John Gordon, an amnesty which left them in possession of their lands and properties.

John died in 1757, leaving Frances with a large family to bring up. Their eldest son, Alexander, followed the Jacobite tradition in seeking service abroad, but was arrested on suspicion of being a spy and beheaded at Brest in 1769. Little was ever ascertained regarding the background to this affair, but in later years several pretenders to his name and estates appeared, although none succeeded in convincing the family. John's second son, not surprisingly named Charles Edward, was placed under the guardianship of a member of the Duke of Gordon's family and, perhaps with a view to correcting the Jacobite influence, received his education at Marischal College, Aberdeen. This, however, did not prevent him from marrying Charlotte Boyd, the daughter of the Hon. Charles Boyd, a prominent Jacobite exile and the son of Lord Kilmarnock, in 1773. The couple had one son and two daughters, but the marriage was to be tragically short, for Charlotte died in 1778, it was said 'from the effects of cold caught after over-heating herself in dancing'.

Charles married again on 5 December 1781, his second wife being Katherine Mercer, the elder daughter of Major James Mercer of Achnacant, and Katherine Douglas, whose beauty was celebrated in more than one Scottish song. James was born on 6 October 1782, and was joined in due course by three brothers and three sisters.

James appears to have inherited the principal characteristics of his grandmothers, for he possessed both Katherine Douglas' looks and Frances' spirit. There was a wildness about him which was much appreciated by Major Mercer, who always welcomed his visits. He seemed to have no fear of heights and was much given to jumping from upper windows until the children's nurse forbade it on the grounds that it set a dangerous example to his younger brothers. He also inherited much of his character from his father with whom he spent a great deal of time. At one stage of his life Charles Gordon had been in the Honourable East India Company's Naval Service and he always retained a great interest in ships and the sea. Whenever he visited Aberdeen on business and was accompanied by James he was able to point out the various types of vessel in harbour and explain the working of their rigging. By now, even the least pragmatic of Jacobites had been forced to admit that the Stuart cause was irrevocably lost and come to terms with life as it was. During the War of American Independence Charles held a Captain's commission in the Gordon Fencibles, a unit raised by the Duke and Duchess of Gordon.[1] On 8 July 1778 he was leading a recruiting party at St Sairs Fair when he was attacked by a rival party under Captain Alexander Davidson, which was drumming up support for the same regiment. Next day he wrote to the Duke of Gordon:

'Fordyce, your Grace's piper, had his pipes broke at the head of the party by some riotous people. I was several times struck at with a bludgeon by a servant of Captain Davidson, an active hand seemingly in the fray; and at the same time Mr Leith received a severe wound on the head from one of the party. We, however, got both the men secured who struck at him and me, and considered it as a proper measure to carry them instantly before Captain Davidson as the only Justice of the Peace then in the market, to be dealt with according to their offence. But to our surprise he not only refused to act or to take any concern in the matter, but after being put in mind by Mr Leith that his duty as a magistrate demanded his interference, he answered that he was not responsible to him for his conduct. I cannot help thinking but that the abuse and indignity calls for the strictest enquiry and chastisement. Leith's blood was running to his heels.'

His Grace, unfortunately, was not inclined to intervene in a dispute between his officers. Charles was subsequently informed that his assailants, having fallen out among themselves that very night, had beaten the daylights out of each other, and with that he had to be content.

On the outbreak of the war with Revolutionary France in January 1793 he again put on scarlet, this time as Captain and Paymaster in the North Fencibles. When his family, now living in their partially completed new home on the Wardhouse estate, visited him in the Fencibles' camp, James and his brothers amused themselves among the regiment's drummers, some of whom would certainly be known to them. The upshot was that James became a competent drummer with a knowledge of all the calls, a skill which, quite shortly, was to lead him to a most unwelcome prominence.

Some discussion had already begun among the family as to what career James was follow. At about the time of his eleventh birthday a letter was received from Lord Glenbervie, who was married to his aunt Katherine. It seemed that a friend of Katherine's, Captain James Whitshed, RN, had just commissioned *Arrogant* (74) at Chatham, where she was presently fitting out, and would be happy to take any young friend of hers to sea with him.

The offer was accepted with alacrity, and if today it might seem heartless to pack off an eleven-year-old to the hard life of the sea, with a real prospect of battle and violent death in the immediate offing, two hundred years ago that was certainly not the case. Indeed a great deal of thought went into the decision and the family believed, quite correctly, that they were acting in James's best interests. The fact was that the Royal Navy was a very professional service in which achieving commissioned rank and subsequent promotion was governed by strict rules. Looked at through the wrong end of the telescope, one could only become an admiral if one had acquired sufficient seniority on the Captains' List; as a captain, too, one was entitled to the lion's share of any prize money won by his ship, and captain was thus the key rank to be aimed for as early as possible. But promotion from lieutenant to captain was not always easy, nor was it always fair. A lieutenant could obtain promotion by distinguished service or by bringing himself to the attention of his superiors in other ways, or by the influence of patrons who were either themselves serving senior officers or who were able to exert pressure on the Admiralty. The system was far from perfect, but it was more logical than that of the Army, in which commissions and promotion were purchased, sometimes resulting in the elevation of quite unsuitable individuals to senior ranks. Furthermore, the Navy's system kept out dilettanti and time wasters like George 'Beau' Brummel, since a man could not even sit the examination for lieutenant until he had spent six years at sea, including three as a midshipman or master's mate. If, on entering the Navy, a candidate was too young for a midshipman's berth, he would be mustered as a 'captain's servant' until he was old enough, though in 1794 the system was altered slightly in that only boys aged eleven and over were accepted, being designated as Volunteers Class I and paid at the rate of £6 per annum. Even so, such a boy required a personal or family acquaintance with the ship's captain before he could be enrolled. In entering James for the Royal Navy, therefore, the Gordon family must have felt that he would have a secure future. If all went well, he would pass the examination for lieutenant when he was seventeen or eighteen and attain the rank of captain while in his twenties; furthermore, he enjoyed the patronage of the Glenbervies. Obviously, they could not have foreseen that the United Kingdom was about to embark on what is now regarded as the first of the World Wars, which was to go on for nearly twenty-two years. On the other hand the country had been at war with France more or less continuously throughout the previous century so fighting the French had almost become a natural condition of life.

While Captain Gordon was away with the Fencibles, a tutor named Cruikshank had been appointed to oversee the children's education. Sadly, he lacked the ability to impart knowledge, and this was to have unfortunate consequences for the eldest of his charges in a year or two's time. James, who was undoubtedly a handful, described him as being 'not one of the best-tempered men in the world', but was honest enough to confess that he himself was 'rather an obstinate sort of chap'. The inevitable confrontation ended with Cruikshank trying to flog James, who, determined that he should not do so, was thrown down in the ensuing struggle and temporarily dislocated his jaw.

Even in his later years, James vividly remembered hearing the news that he was to go to sea. The family was then at Gordon Hall and James recalled that it was a Sunday afternoon and that one of them was reading a sermon.

'We heard a coach drive up to the door; we all started to see who it was when out came Aunt Peggy. When a little composed, she told us she had come to take me away, as I was to be sent to sea to fight the French, and that we should leave home early in the morning. Of course, such information gave me great pleasure, as it would take me away from school. I had certainly seen the sea and had often been on board ship in the harbour of Aberdeen. When at home I usually slept with my brother Robert, who was only five years old at this time, but as it was the last night I got leave to sleep with Sylvester, my next brother, eight years old. We did not sleep much, as you may suppose; we were building castles in the air till nearly daylight. Mr Cruikshank, who always slept in the same room with us, took this opportunity to beg me not to inform my father of his conduct to me. I now know I ought to have made him acquainted with his treatment of us, but I never did.'

After calling at the Mercers' James set off for London, escorted by one of his father's Fencibles, a Mr Pell. Their first stop was in Edinburgh where James stayed with his half-sisters Fanny and Jane, causing such uproar that it remained the talk of the family for many years. They next stopped for a week at the home of a Mr Marjoribanks on the Tweed, in which James hooked a salmon so big that it would have pulled him into the water had not adult assistance arrived to help him land it. At length, posting to London, Pell set down his unruly charge at Lord Glenbervie's house in Bedford Square and thankfully returned to Scotland. Word had been received from Captain Witshed that he would not be required to report for a while, so he spent some time there and sometimes accompanied Lord Glenbervie to his country house, The Pheasantry. His behaviour had not improved and he later admitted to being '... as mischievous as a young monkey. Lady Guilford, my aunt's mother, was then alive, and was Ranger of Bushey Park. I was often there and used to play with her daughters, afterwards Lady Sheffield and Lady C. Lindsay, to their great annoyance, I believe.' Captain and Mrs Whitshed called at Bedford Square and, on being presented to them, James was told the date upon which he should join his ship. Despite all the disturbance he caused, he was a likeable lad and before he left Lady Glenbervie and Lady Guilford each presented him with a guinea. This newly acquired wealth was promptly spent on the unauthorised purchase of a horse-pistol.

Lord Glenbervie had him driven down to Chatham in his carriage, accompanied by a servant to help him with his sea chest. On the way, the servant made a remarkably prescient observation to him: 'In a few years' time I dare say you will be driving down here in a carriage of your own, instead of your uncle's.' At first James lived at the Whitsheds' lodgings with them and was mothered by their landlady, Mrs Hulbert, when they were away.

Every captain of a newly commissioned ship faced the twin difficulties of getting the dockyard to complete the necessary work and mustering a crew, and Captain Whitshed was no exception. In due course both processes became sufficiently far advanced for James to move aboard the accommodation hulk moored alongside *Arrogant*, which provided temporary housing for the ship's officers and men. He was housed in the Gunroom under the care of the Gunner, sharing the berth with the warrant officers and another Volunteer Class 1 of the same age who was the First Lieutenant's son. While checking the new arrival's sea chest, the Purser, Mr Burnet, was horrified to discover the horse-pistol, which he promptly returned to the gunsmith before any mischief could be done, retaining the money on trust to prevent a similar purchase.

During the day, James attended school in Rochester, returning to the hulk at night. The total lack of privacy, the overcrowding, the constant noise and movement of shipboard life, even aboard a hulk, does not seem to have bothered him in the least. During the early days, simply understanding what was going on must have been difficult, despite such knowledge as had been imparted by his father. Nautical terms apart, language presented its own problems, as the seamen's oaths were – and remain – entirely in a class of their own with many of the same words doing duty as noun, verb, adjective and adverb. The hierarchic nature of the life, too, must have been difficult for him to interpret. The positions of the officers and petty officers were, of course, clearly defined, but less intelligible was the pecking order among the seamen, especially as they wore no uniforms or badges of rank.[2] When everyone looked alike, it took time to sort out who were the really important members of the crew, like the topmen, and those – like the landsmen – whose only importance lay in their presence.

Not that James at this juncture had remotely absorbed the concept of a carefully structured, disciplined service; the Royal Navy was, quite simply, fun. Under-employed, he and the First Lieutenant's son teamed up with the ship's boys, about twenty in number, who taught them the finer points of swearing. James referred to them as 'blackguards', which meant, in his language, that they were game for anything, preferably illegal, and indeed he used the same term about himself. Not unnaturally the boys were happy to follow the lead of an errant Volunteer Class I, especially one who displayed some powers of leadership. At night the gang would obtain lights and steal from the hulk into *Arrogant* alongside, sometimes coming dangerously close to setting the ship ablaze. There they hunted rats with harpoons and threw them overboard.[3] Some of the boys also stole pieces of lead and other sundries left about by the dockyard workers, selling them ashore. This did not interest James greatly, who was to comment throughout his life that he 'never cared for money, never had any, and never wanted it'!

At length *Arrogant* was ready for sea. The crew settled in and the Marine detachment, about 100 strong and smart in their scarlet and pipeclay, came aboard.[4] Their role as sea soldiers was explained to James, as was the reason for their being quartered between the officers and seamen, namely that they were 'sworn men' who stood guard over the former's quarters and elsewhere throughout the ship and enforced regulations regarding conduct among the seamen.

The excitement of setting sail had barely subsided when James found himself up to his neck in trouble. He always remained a little diffident about what happened, telling his daughters that as there was no one on board who could beat the drum, he had the honour of beating to quarters the first night, but as the captain did not think it necessary that he should be a performer, he threatened to have him flogged. Reading between the lines, this has only a partial ring of truth about it. The establishment of the Marine detachment aboard a Seventy-four included one and possibly two drummers, and the presence of a drum aboard also suggests the presence of an owner. It therefore seems not unlikely that James, recalling his visits to the Fencibles, quickly made himself known to the Marine drummer. Anxious to expand his repertoire, he asked to be shown how to beat to quarters, and the drummer tapped out the call on the rim. To the drummer's horror, the eleven-year-old Mr Gordon then actually beat the call, with the result that over 600 men erupted into action all over the ship, tables and partitions vanished as if by magic, gunports swung open, squealing gun carriages rumbled inboard ready for loading, startled officers came running from their cabins, and Captain Whitshed demanded furiously to know what was going on. A moment's incredulous silence was followed, for James, by the unpleasant discovery that Captain Whitshed afloat could be terrible in his wrath. He was not flogged, of course, but he was almost certainly required to 'kiss the Gunner's daughter', that is, receive a good spanking from the gunner while straddling a gun in the Gunroom. Whitshed also gave him such a roasting that he reflected ruefully in middle age, 'I have never attempted to play on any instrument since.[5]

The Seventy-fours were the Navy's backbone, forming the majority in the line of battle and also in the squadrons which blockaded an enemy's coast-line. During *Arrogant*'s shake-down cruise, which took place off the Texel, Whitshed exercised his officers and crew regularly in all aspects of seamanship, clearing for action and gunnery, bringing them to an acceptable standard of efficiency. James, as well as being assigned regular duties, also began his formal training. This generally took the form of a different class held each afternoon except Sunday, involving both the younger midshipmen and the Volunteers Class I. One day they would go aloft, quite literally learning the ropes; next, learning how to knot and splice under the boatswain; next, how to cast the lead; next, navigation and log-keeping under the Master or his mates; next, signalling under the yeoman; next, smallarms handling under the Marine sergeant; next, gun drill under the gunner; next, seamanship, again under the Master; and so on, until the lessons were driven home by constant repetition. There was much to learn but, sadly, James was not a good pupil.

At the end of the cruise *Arrogant* was ordered to join the Channel Fleet and sailed for Portsmouth. There she was met by the unusual sight of French warships lying at anchor at Spithead, flying not the revolutionary tricolour but the golden lilies of the Bourbons. Aboard were a large number of Royalist refugees who had escaped from Toulon in December 1793 when General Jacques Dugomier's revolutionary troops, acting upon a plan prepared by a young artillery colonel named Napoleon Bonaparte, had stormed the defences of the port.

On 2 May 1794 *Arrogant* and five other ships of the line left Spithead as escort for the East and West Indies and Newfoundland convoys. These were seen clear of the Channel and then, once the convoys had reached the point at which their courses diverged, the squadron turned back, reaching Plymouth towards the end of May. As the French were reported to be at sea in strength, the squadron was reinforced with three more ships of the line and a frigate, and immediately dispatched to join Admiral Lord Howe and the Channel Fleet. Unfortunately it did not find Howe until the day after his victory on what became known as The Glorious First of June, but James's recollection of subsequent events remained vivid.

'We chased five French men-of-war into a port near Brest, and the next morning fell in with the disabled French fleet. Unfortunately, we did not attack them. If we had I thought we might have taken or destroyed the whole of them; they had lost their masts a few days before in the actions of the 29th May and 1st June. I was a boy of twelve, and of course could not know much about it, and as I never heard that our Admiral was found fault with, I must have been mistaken. We went to Plymouth, and from thence to Spithead, where we found the ships' crews which had been in action in high spirits – they would hardly deign to speak to fellows in our squadron.'

There followed a prolonged period of blockade duty off Brest and elsewhere with little of note happening and an endlessly boring routine of tacking, going about and changing sail in accordance with the weather, the major problems for the crews being how to keep out the cold and stay dry as one Atlantic storm after another came in from the west. The crew of *Arrogant* were not sorry to be recalled to port in February 1795, but sailed shortly after in company with most of Lord Howe's fleet to escort an enormous convoy clear of the Channel. The escort alone numbered 43 ships of the line, 34 frigates and other armed vessels, and a Portuguese squadron of five sail of the line, one frigate and two brigs. The convoy itself numbered no less than 500 merchantmen, covering the sea from horizon to horizon. It was, James thought, 'a fine sight'.

On *Arrogant*'s return to Spithead, Captain Whitshed was ordered to prepare the ship for service in the East India Squadron. This he probably regarded as being a backwater in which he would be removed from the mainstream of naval life and, having sufficient seniority and influence to obtain another command fairly quickly, he decided to relinquish *Arrogant*. Before leaving, however, he gave some thought to James's future. It was important that there should be no break in the boy's sea service, and he believed that he would probably benefit from the livelier life of a frigate. He therefore made arrangements for him to be transferred to *Eurydice*, commanded by a personal friend, Captain Francis Cole.

Eurydice was at sea, and while awaiting her arrival James was accommodated first in *Ramillies* (Captain Sir Richard Bickerton), then in *Invincible* (Captain the Hon. Thomas Packenham) and then in *Defence* (Captain Thomas Wells), all Seventy-Fours taking their turn in harbour. For the first time in his life, James, having just lost his first shipmates and now embarked upon the difficult process of growing up, began to feel isolated and in low spirits.

'At this time of my life I was a complete blackguard. I never wrote home, because I could not write, nor do I remember ever receiving a letter from any of my relations. At last I joined the *Eurydice* and was happy to find mids of my own age on board; they were all fine, smart boys and good sailors. I was soon ashamed of myself and now began to pay attention to my profession.'

James joined *Eurydice* at Plymouth whence she escorted a convoy up-Channel to Portsmouth. There, as a mark of favour, Cole was offered command of the larger, more powerful frigate *Révolutionnaire*, which had recently been captured from the French. Naturally he accepted and his crew turned over with him. The frigate's rigging had been badly cut up during her capture and Cole, a fair man but a hard taskmaster, made all his midshipmen and younger volunteers work aloft and assist in the re-rigging. James commented that while the experience did everyone a great deal of good, it left them covered with tar.

In June 1795 *Révolutionnaire* sailed as part of Admiral Lord Bridport's squadron, consisting of fourteen ships of the line, eight of which were three-deckers, and several frigates. On 22 June a French squadron of twelve ships of the line and eleven smaller vessels, commanded by Admiral Villaret de Joyeuse, was sighted. The French Navy had purged most of its officers in a frenzy of revolutionary fervour and replaced them with men drawn from the merchant service who, though able enough seamen, had little or no knowledge of naval administration, tactics or gunnery. Furthermore, its crews were inexperienced because they spent so much of their time in harbour and the condition of its ships had deteriorated as a result of mismanagement within the dockyards and the fact that in France the Navy, being the junior service, was allocated fewer resources. Villaret was one of his Navy's most successful commanders. It is true that, tactically, he had been defeated during the Glorious First of June, but in the wider strategic sense his responsibility had been to escort a large grain convoy from America, and most of this had reached port safely. Again, less than a fortnight before Bridport's sails came over the horizon, he had chased off a small British squadron blockading Brest.

Now, knowing the condition of his ships and seeing that the odds were approximately even, he sought to avoid action and turned away, heading for Lorient. Bridport pursued, but the winds were light and even with all sails set the gap between the two squadrons obstinately refused to close. The pursuit continued throughout the night, but during the following morning the leading eight of Bridport's heavy ships came up with those at the rear of the French line, taking three of them. By now Villaret and the remaining nine were already in the approaches to Lorient and were positioned inshore of the Ile de Groix, waiting for a tide in order to enter the harbour. With the benefit of hindsight, critics were to suggest that Bridport should have followed them, but, knowing that the coastline abounded in treacherous shoals and rocks, and lacking adequate charts of the area, he decided not to risk turning a tangible success into a potential disaster.

One of the prizes taken during Bridport's Action, as the engagement came to be known, was a former British ship of the line, the *Alexander*, which had been captured by the French the previous November. As Révolutionnaire had sprung her main mast during the pursuit she was given the task of towing the dismasted *Alexander* into Plymouth harbour, where she was received by cheering crowds.

Little of note took place in the Channel for the remainder of the year. Both sides concentrated on the destruction of each other's commerce and Révolutionnaire was engaged on routine convoy escort or blockade duties.

It was in March 1796 that Captain Cole sent for James, who had now spent almost three years at sea, the minimum period required before he could be considered for a midshipman's berth. As kindly as possible, Cole told him that there were occasions in the service when the responsibilities thrust upon a midshipman were very heavy indeed for a young man, not least being the lives of the men placed under his command. Because of this he hoped that James would understand that, since he remained only semi-literate, he could not be recommended for promotion. In the circumstances, therefore, Cole continued, James should seriously consider whether his future lay within the Royal Navy and, so that he could discuss the matter with his family, he would grant leave for that purpose.

Having, as he believed, really made an effort since he came under Cole's command, James felt shocked, ill-used and resentful. He went to the Glenbervies' in London, where the crisis led to a family conference attended by his mother, so seriously ill that this was the last time he saw her, and by his Uncle Mercer. It was decided to invoke the assistance of Captain Whitshed, now commanding *Namur* (90), who agreed to have James back, though he made no promises as to his future, which would lie in the boy's own hands. The episode provides a minor if interesting example of the use of influence within the Royal Navy. In the years to come, though the Glenbervies would continue to support James's interest whenever the occasion offered, this was to be the last occasion upon which their assistance was to be needed; having put his awkward years behind him, henceforth he would make steady and sustained progress by his own efforts.

NOTES

1. Fencibles, as the name suggests, were a home defence force intended to support the Militia. England, Wales, Ireland and the Isle of Man all had Militia units liable for mobilisation, but Scotland had no Militia and therefore raised the highest proportion of Fencible units in the United Kingdom during the dangerous years between 1793 and 1802 – fourteen out of 30 cavalry regiments and 44 out of 68 infantry regiments.

2. Although some captains fitted out their gigs' crews at their own expense, there was no official uniform for seamen below the rank of petty officer before 1857.

3. Forester had obviously read of this and used a version of the game in 'The Man Who Saw God' (*Mr Midshipman Hornblower*), in which young Hornblower nervously exercises his authority for the first time to stop illegal gambling in the cable tier. The gamblers included some of the ship's senior hands, bets being made on how many rats certain individuals could kill with their teeth alone.

4. The professional corps of Marines, as opposed to soldiers drafted for service at sea, did not receive the distinction of Royal until 1802.

5. Such anecdotes are grist to the writer's mill, but Forester was obviously unable to use this episode as the young Mr Hornblower was something of an introspective sobersides. However, whereas Gordon forswore musical instruments for life after his tongue-lashing from Whitshed, Forester used his fondness for the drum to flesh out Hornblower's character. Thus, in 'The Frogs and the Lobsters' (*Mr Midshipman Hornblower*), dealing with British support for a French Royalist landing on the coast of Brittany, Hornblower was greatly impressed by a squad of drummers beating Reveille. 'Hornblower, tone-deaf but highly sensitive to rhythm, thought it was fine music, real music,' wrote Forester.

Chapter 2
FLEET ACTIONS AND PROMOTION

James joined the *Namur* in May 1796 and was pleased to find a number of familiar faces aboard. Further blockade duties in the Channel followed and in December these were extended to the Irish coast, a French invasion force numbering 43 warships and transports, with 15,000 troops aboard, having broken out of Brest with the object of landing in Ireland to support a planned rebellion. Gales scattered the French and although some of their ships succeeded in entering Bantry Bay further foul weather prevented a landing. Finally the project was abandoned and the force returned to Brest, having lost five ships to the storms and six captured.

Meanwhile the strategic balance of the war had altered dramatically. Spain, originally a supporter of the First Coalition against Revolutionary France, changed sides on 19 August. This seriously threatened the British position in the Mediterranean, from which it was decided to withdraw temporarily. The islands of Corsica and Elba were evacuated and the Mediterranean Fleet, commanded by Admiral Sir John Jervis, was forced to abandon its blockade of Toulon and retire to Gibraltar. The real danger now was that if the French and Dutch fleets, the latter now being under French control, were joined by the Spaniards in the Channel, their combined strength would amount to approximately sixty ships of the line, against which the Channel Fleet could, perhaps, muster a maximum of forty.

The most important task facing Jervis, therefore, was to contain the Spaniards. This was more easily said than done, for accidents had reduced his strength to ten ships of the line. To assist him the Admiralty dispatched five more, including *Namur*, in January 1797. Calling briefly at Lisbon, the reinforcements learned that Jervis was off Cape St Vincent and joined him there on 6 February.

Jervis' principal concern was that the Spaniards might slip past him undetected, but in the event the winds conspired to bring them straight to him. When the Spanish fleet left its Mediterranean base at Cartagena on 1 February its commander, Admiral José de Cordoba, intended to pass through the Straits of Gibraltar and put in at Cadiz before continuing north to join the French. But a continuous strong easterly wind blew his fleet far out into the Atlantic before veering round to the west, making it inevitable that the next leg of its passage would bring it into contact with the waiting British ships.

Its approach was signalled during the night of 13/14 February by gun signals, this being the means by which stragglers were kept in contact with the main body of a fleet during the hours of darkness. The Spaniards' lights became visible before dawn and as their topsails broke the horizon south-west of the British fleet it became clear that they were on a course from west to east. It also became clear that Jervis was outnumbered by almost two to one. The story has it that as more and more ships of the line were sighted Jervis, pacing his quarterdeck, passed little comment until the number reached twenty-seven, when he snapped tartly at his informant: 'Enough, sir! If there are fifty sail of the line, I shall go through them!'

And that is exactly what he did. He had noticed that the Spaniards were sailing in two untidy, separate groups, with seven ships in the van and twenty in the rear. His own fleet was now bearing down in line-ahead from the north-east and he decided to penetrate the gap and engage the Spanish rear, fifteen ships against twenty, calculating that it would take the enemy van considerable time to come about and beat to windward before it could join the action. The British line was led by *Culloden*, with Jervis in the centre aboard the 100-gun *Victory* and, third from the rear, Captain Horatio Nelson, flying his commodore's pennant in *Captain* (74).

Once *Culloden* was well into the gap, Jervis gave the order to tack in succession, which would bring his line parallel with that of Córdoba's as the British caught up. The Spaniards were now on a north-north-easterly course, but Nelson suddenly noticed that their leading ship, the 132-gun *Santissima Trinidad*, then the largest warship afloat, had again changed her heading and, with the wind directly astern, was striving to close the gap between the two groups. Ignoring the tack in succession order, he swung *Captain* out of the line, followed by the two ships astern, in a successful bid to head her off. Jervis, reading his thoughts, condoned his action with the signal 'each ship to take suitable station and engage as arriving in succession'. The engagement then became general, save for the Spanish van, which made no attempt to intervene.

This was James's baptism of fire. True, he had seen casualties and shattered ships before, but until now his own ship had only played a peripheral part in events. He says nothing of what he did aboard *Namur*, but he was almost certainly employed as a messenger by one of the officers. The sheer volume of noise, with hundreds of guns firing, gun carriages rumbling and squealing, the crash and clatter of falling rigging, shouted commands and the screams of injured men, was a physical shock in itself. Likewise, his mind had to absorb the horrors of roundshot cutting men in two, beheading them or ripping their limbs off, as well as the agony of seamen blinded or impaled by flying splinters of wood. There was, too, the continuous physical destruction of apparently solid objects on both sides – stout bulwarks shattered, thick masts shot through until they crashed over the side, and heavy guns overturned in a trice. From the older hands he would already have learned what to expect and that, whatever was going on around him, he should concentrate his mind entirely on whatever job he had been given. He would have noticed that the gun crews, some stripped to the waist and with sweatbands around their heads, went about their work with fierce pleasure, heaving their charges in and out, loading, ramming, firing and sponging as fast as possible in accordance with the drill they had practised so many times; and that, while many of the Spanish ships carried far more guns than *Namur*, the rate of fire maintained by their less experienced crews was slower than that of the British, who were getting off ten shots to their six or seven; and also that because of this the enemy – clearly seen because the battle was being fought point-blank, the opposing ships mere yards apart – were being savagely punished.[1]

The battle, which was to take its name from Cape St Vincent, had begun at about noon. By three, those ships of the enemy rear which could had broken clear of the mêlée and were heading for the Spanish coast. They left behind them in British hands the *San Isidró* (74), *San Nicolás* (84), *San José* (112), and *Salvador del Mundo* (112); the great *Santissima Trinidad* had also struck her colours but made off before it was possible to take possession of her. Jervis was rewarded for his victory with an earldom, taking the title St Vincent. Nelson's seamanship during the battle, including the boarding in succession of *San Nicholás* and *San José*, won him a knighthood and promotion to Rear-Admiral.

Rallied, Córdoba's fleet remained in the offing and next day seemed willing to renew the contest. The odds against the British remained much the same – 23 ships against twelve, *Captain* being so badly damaged that she was under tow, and two more of Jervis' fleet were no longer fit for action – but many Spanish ships also had serious damage to repair and, distrusting the ability of his inexperienced crews to perform fleet manoeuvres, Córdoba thought better of the idea and retired into Cadiz, which was promptly blockaded when further reinforcements arrived from the Channel Fleet.

James emerged unharmed from his ordeal, but his brief autobiographical notes tell us very little: 'We were particularly engaged with the

Salvador del Mundo and took her in tow next day. On the 16th we anchored in Lagos Bay (Portugal), where we nearly lost all our prizes in a gale of wind. I was employed in landing the prisoners and was on shore during the gale. By the 23rd we had all our ships and prizes in order and sailed for Lisbon, arriving on the 28th. After we had refitted we sailed with the Fleet to blockade Cadiz.'

He recalled that one night what he described as two Spanish 'galleons' sailed through the blockading squadron and that one of them actually hailed *Namur* without attracting undue interest. The Spanish economy was still supported by shipments of minted gold and silver from Spain's South and Central American colonies and it was the ambition of every captain and crew to capture such a vessel. When daylight revealed the nature of the two strangers, therefore, they were promptly pursued. But the Spaniards were almost home, and one ran herself ashore while the other managed to get much of her precious cargo away in her boats before she was captured.

During this period Captain Whitshed obtained leave to return home and sent his boys to serve under another old friend, Captain Thomas Foley, who had recently been given command of *Goliath* (74).[2] This proved to be a major turning point in James's career because, whereas Whitshed was largely prepared to let the young men work out their own salvation, Foley took a personal interest in them. Of him James commented, 'He always behaved so much like a father to us all, that I consider myself to be under great obligations to him.' It was at once apparent to Foley why James, a likeable, intelligent lad still filled with enthusiasm for the Service, was making so little headway in his career, and he decided to correct the fault. The establishment of a 74 provided for a schoolmaster, and in *Goliath* it was a Mr Strachan, who was instructed to bring James's literacy up to the required standard. This he succeeded in doing and in due course James received his longed-for promotion to the midshipmen's berth, although he does not say exactly when.

As James recalls, during the summer months the blockade of Cadiz was an active rather than a passive affair. 'As we belonged to the inshore squadron, we were often in action with the forts and gunboats. On the 5th of July at night we went in to cover the bomb-ships and boats, which made an attack on Cadiz under the command of Lord [*sic*] Nelson. I never saw such firing – few shots struck us though many went over us – and we lost no men. Lord Nelson in his barge fell in with the Spanish commanding officer – he had 26 men of whom eighteen were killed and the rest wounded.[3] Two of the Spanish gunboats were taken on the 5th July. We remained at anchor off Cadiz until the winter gales obliged us to keep well offshore. A part of the fleet was sent to Lisbon to refit; we were one of the ships, but the Spanish fleet came out, chased our squadron that had been left at Cadiz, and we sailed after having been only four days in port. Just as we got in sight of Cadiz we saw the Spaniards going back into port.'

Elsewhere, the year 1797 had seen momentous events taking place within the Royal Navy. On 15 April Lord Bridport's Channel Fleet, anchored at Spithead, mutinied. The men's grievances included bad food resulting from corrupt practices within the victualling service; poor pay, which was but a quarter of that which could be obtained in the merchant service and which, unbelievably, had not been increased since the reign of Charles II; delay in the distribution of prize money; disgraceful conditions endured by the wounded and sick; and lack of shore leave. In every case, the seamen had genuine cause for complaint, and they affirmed their loyalty by promising to return to duty if the French put to sea. In its wisdom the government appointed Admiral Lord Howe, whom the seamen trusted, to deal with them, and their demands, including a pardon for those involved, were met within a week. Hardly had the Channel Fleet put to sea again when, on 20 May, Admiral Adam Duncan's North Sea Fleet, stationed at the Nore, mutinied. Most of the men remained good-hearted but they were influenced by sea-lawyers keen to exploit further the concessions that had been made, and the manner in which the mutiny was organised had recognisable revolutionary undertones. The principal task of the North Sea Fleet was to keep Admiral Jan de Winter's Dutch fleet penned within the Texel, and there was every chance that once de Winter became aware of the prevailing situation he would sally out to join the French. The situation was saved by Duncan himself, who had personally quelled the mutiny aboard his own flagship, the *Venerable*, and one other ship, *Adamant*. Together, these two remained off the Texel, sending signals to an imaginary fleet below the horizon, and the Dutch remained where they were. By 10 June the mutiny had begun to crumble and four days later it collapsed. This time, the Admiralty being in no mood to grant further concessions, some of the ringleaders were hanged and the rest flogged round the fleet and imprisoned.

Yet it was this same fleet which gave the Royal Navy its next major victory. On 7 October de Winter, with fifteen ships of the line, emerged from the Texel. Duncan, with sixteen ships in two columns, broke the enemy line four days later off Camperdown and a fiercely contested mêlée ensued. The Dutch put up an unbelievably stubborn fight but after three and a half hours of close action, in which the heavy shot thrown by the British carronades proved decisive, nine of their ships had hauled down their colours.[4] It is a measure of the ferocity of the fight that the prizes were so badly damaged that they remained good only for their raw materials.

Thus the year saw the removal of the invasion threat to Great Britain posed by a possible concentration of Franco–Spanish–Dutch naval might, leaving her free to pursue wider strategic aims. The same, of course, was true of France, where the Directory in Paris had become seriously alarmed by the meteoric career of Napoleon Bonaparte, now a full general. Bonaparte was successful, popular, ruthless, possessed of a burning ambition and thus an extremely dangerous man; it would, in the Directory's eyes, be a very good idea if he were employed as far away from France as possible. It was, therefore, with considerable pleasure that it approved an idea submitted by Bonaparte himself, namely that he should lead an expedition to Egypt, thereby simultaneously creating a French sphere of influence in the Middle East and a stepping-stone to India with the long-term objective of ruining British trade in both areas. In April 1798 he was appointed commander of the 40,000-strong Army of the Orient, which began assembling at Toulon, where the French Mediterranean Fleet, commanded by Vice-Admiral François Brueys, was putting its ships in order and assembling the large number of transports required.

The unusual degree of activity in the Toulon area was reported simultaneously by British intelligence sources both to Lord St Vincent off Cadiz and to the British government in London. On 2 May, acting on his own initiative, St Vincent detached Rear-Admiral Sir Horatio Nelson, with three ships of the line and four frigates, to find out what was happening. On the same day the Cabinet sent instructions to St Vincent, requiring him to dispatch part of his fleet and destroy the French expedition, wherever it was bound.

Hoisting his flag in *Vanguard* (74), Nelson set sail immediately for Toulon, arriving off the base on 17 May. Two days later his squadron was widely scattered and blown into the Golfe du Lion by a vicious gale lasting two days, during which *Vanguard* sustained such heavy damage to her masts and rigging that she had to be towed to a sheltered anchorage on the south coast of Sardinia to effect repairs. These took only four days to complete, but the frigate captains, believing that Nelson would have headed for Gibraltar, decided to do likewise.

Brueys used the same wind that had scattered Nelson's squadron to get his ships out of harbour. Escorted by thirteen ships of the line and a number of smaller warships, Bonaparte's expedition embarked on the first leg of its voyage, which would take it to Malta. There, the Knights of St John, despite their superb fortifications, had long since ceased to be a military power and they tamely surrendered, enabling a French garrison to take possession of the island.

St Vincent, now in receipt of the cabinet's instructions, dispatched *Goliath* and eight more Seventy-Fours, plus the brig *La Mutine*, under the overall command of Captain Thomas Troubridge, to support Nelson. *La Mutine*, commanded by Captain Thomas Hardy, was sailing ahead of the fleet and, on 2 June, having passed through the Straits, she spoke with one of Nelson's frigates, *Alcmene*, on her way to Gibraltar. Hardy, who was to captain the *Victory* at Trafalgar, followed his instinct and proceeded to the blockade area off Toulon, where he joined Nelson on 5 June. Two days later Troubridge arrived, bringing with him an additional Seventy-Four and a Fifty which he had picked up at Gibraltar. He also brought St Vincent's written orders, requiring Nelson to 'proceed in quest of the Armament [Expedition] prepared by the enemy and to use your utmost endeavours to take, sink, burn or destroy it'.

What were the French up to and, more importantly, where had they gone? Three possibilities suggested themselves: the economically important West Indies, Ireland, or the eastern Mediterranean. Nelson was dubious about the first two and uncertain regarding the third.[5] His problems were aggravated by his total lack of frigates which normally served as the eyes of the fleet. He proceeded down the coasts of Italy and Sicily without being any the wiser, but off Malta he learned that the French, having taken the island, had left three days earlier. Fragmentary evidence suggested that they had sailed east, and Nelson reached the correct conclusion that they were heading for Alexandria. He sailed there immediately, but found no trace of them. He then turned north to reconnoitre the Turkish coast and, again finding nothing, returned to Sicily.

He had missed his quarry because Brueys, instead of taking the direct course for Alexandria, had paused off the south coast of Crete to allow stragglers among the slow transports to catch up. The Expedition reached Alexandria on 1 July and the following day Bonaparte stormed the city. He then marched up the Nile and on 21 July defeated a 60,000-strong Mameluke army at the Battle of the Pyramids, taking possession of Cairo.[6] So far his grand design was proceeding entirely to plan.

Still convinced that Brueys was somewhere in the eastern Mediterranean, Nelson again reversed course and had paused to re-victual off the southern coast of Greece, then ruled by Turkey, when he received the information he needed. Troubridge, commanding *Culloden*, put in at the little mainland harbour of Kuroni on 28 July and was told by Turkish officials that the French were in Alexandria.

The fleet sailed for Egypt at once. When it arrived off Alexandria during the morning of 1 August the harbour was indeed crowded with transports but of Brueys' warships there was no sign. It was believed that they might be occupying the alternative anchorage of Aboukir Bay, some ten miles to the east and close to the Nile Delta, and this was confirmed during the afternoon. By evening Nelson's fleet had closed up and was ready to attack.

The wind was from the north-west and Brueys had anchored his major units in a single defensive line protected, he hoped, by shoal water on all but the seaward side; his frigates, bomb vessels and gunboats, drawing less water, were anchored closer inshore. The appearance of the British seems to have taken him by surprise, for a proportion of his crews were still ashore and his decks remained cluttered from the disembarkation of the expeditionary force. Even so, he believed that his opponents' only course of action would be to close with his line from seaward and, as the two fleets were of equal strength, he expected his ships to give them a very hot reception indeed.

Nelson's first intention had been simply to concentrate on the half dozen ships at the head of the enemy line, knowing that the contrary wind would prevent the rest intervening for some considerable time. Aboard *Goliath*, however, Foley had noticed that the French ships, lying with their heads to the wind, were anchored by the bow only. No captain would have dropped anchor without ensuring that there was sufficient room for his ship to swing in any direction when the wind changed, and it followed that where there was room for one ship to swing there was room for another of similar size to pass. If, therefore, the British fleet passed down both sides of the enemy line, this would mean that each French ship in turn would be subjected to the concentrated fire of at least two British ships, and as no warship afloat carried sufficient crew to man her port and starboard batteries simultaneously, the French would be overwhelmed in detail.

The account of the battle left by Midshipman James Gordon tells us nothing of his own part in it and is simply a statement of the salient facts. He was now serving as a Master's mate and was therefore engaged in the sailing and navigation of *Goliath*. In this battle accurate navigation was to be critical and Foley had a distinct advantage in that while the British charts used by his fellow captains were sketchy, he possessed a French chart on which the shoals were more clearly marked.

As the British approached, they were engaged at long range by *Le Guerrier* and *Conquérant*, at the head of the French line, and by the guns on an island at the western end of the bay. Foley was determined to be first inshore of the French and he successfully raced Captain Samuel Hood in *Zealous* for the privilege, raking *Le Guerrier* with a full broadside as he did so. He had intended anchoring alongside his victim but there was a delay in letting go and his ship still had sufficient way to carry her level with *Conquérant*'s afterbody. At this stage *Goliath*, now fully engaged with her second opponent, also came under fire from the frigate *Sérieuse*, moored inshore. Frigates, lacking the thicker sides and hitting power of their larger sisters, normally stayed well clear of actions between ships of the line, but in this case the captain of *Sérieuse*, clearly seeing that disaster was about to overtake the French fleet, obviously felt that he must do what he could to retrieve the situation. Foley was outraged by what he regarded as a piece of the most arrant cheek, bellowing, 'Sink the brute! What does he here?'

Zealous had also now rounded the head of the French line, dropping anchor alongside *Le Guerrier*. Next came *Orion*, continuing down the line to engage *Peuple Souverain*. On the way she passed between *Goliath* and *Sérieuse*, treating the latter to a full broadside, the effect of which was to turn the frigate into a sinking wreck. And so it continued, with more British ships now converging on the seaward side of the French. At length, all of Nelson's Seventy-Fours were engaged save *Culloden*, which had grounded on a shoal at the entrance to the bay; Troubridge declined towing assistance from *Leander* (50), which continued into action and penetrated the gap left by *Peuple Souverain*, now drifting inshore after her cable had parted, and began by raking the much larger *Franklin* to port. *Conquérant*, simultaneously battered by *Goliath* and *Audacious*, struck her colours after only twelve minutes, but elsewhere the French fought on with suicidal bravery. Three hours of fighting reduced *Le Guerrier* to a shambles from which only a single gun fired at intervals; at length Hood sent a boat across to her and her surviving officers were persuaded that there was no further point in prolonging the killing. Aboard the 120-gun French flagship, *L'Orient*, Brueys and his flag captain, de Casa Bianca, were both killed during the early stages of the fighting. A major fire then broke out and, spreading rapidly throughout the ship, the flames illuminated the entire scene. At about 9.30 p.m. *L'Orient* blew up with a shattering roar, showering friend and foe alike with blazing wreckage. The captain of the dismasted *Tonnant*, Dupetit-Thouars, though mortally wounded, had himself propped in a bran tub from which he continued to exercise command until he died; his ship, in fact, did not surrender until the morning of 3 August. As the night wore on some of the French ships began to get under way and two of them, *Heureux* and *Mercure*, ran themselves aground in the process. *Goliath*, seeking fresh opponents after the surrender of *Conquérant*, came across them and, in company with *Theseus*, *Alexander* and *Leander*, forced them to strike after a brief exchange of fire. At about this time the night was riven by a second explosion as the surrendered French frigate *Artémise*, set on fire by her crew, who then escaped in their boats, blew up. The same fate awaited the crippled *Timoleon*, although she did not explode until the afternoon of the 3rd. Rear-Admiral Pierre-Charles Villeneuve, commanding the French rear, made good his escape with two ships of the line and two frigates, but for all practical purposes Brueys' fleet had been annihilated; all that remained were a handful of bomb vessels and gunboats moored in the shallows.

British casualties amounted to 218 killed and 617 wounded. Among the latter was Nelson himself, incapacitated temporarily by a head wound. But the Battle of the Nile, as the engagement is now commonly known, had made him a national hero and its effects were far-reaching. It established Great Britain as the dominant power in the Mediterranean and it destroyed Bonaparte's grand strategic design, leaving him isolated in Egypt.[7]

Nelson's fleet remained in the bay for the next two weeks. Three of the prizes were so badly damaged that they were burned where they lay, and the majority of those remaining were of dubious value. There were also numerous prisoners to attend to, some of whom, survivors of the explosion aboard *L'Orient*, were stark naked and had to be kitted out from the slop chest. Midshipman Gordon was saddened to learn that among *Goliath*'s wounded was the school teacher, Mr Strachan, to whom he owed so much. Strachan's hands were badly burned, probably as the result of a powder fire, and the surgeons, having more pressing cases to attend to, had simply bound them up. When the bandages came off it was found that his fingers were stuck together and had to be separated by painful surgery.

'On the 18th August [James's narrative continues] having refitted the ships and prizes, the fleet sailed from the Bay of Aboukir, leaving Captain Hood with four sail of the line and two frigates to blockade the port of Alexandria. The *Goliath* was stationed in Aboukir Bay and on the night of the 25th August our boats cut out a French gun vessel, of three long-pounders and four swivel guns, manned by 70 men, three of whom, with the commander, were killed and ten wounded, under the guns of the Castle of Aboukir; our lieutenant commanding the boats and one man were wounded. Shortly after this, the *Goliath* joined Lord Nelson in the Bay of Naples and was employed there and at the blockade of Malta until the end of 1799.'[8]

On arrival at Portsmouth in December, *Goliath* was paid off. James moved temporarily into the *Royal William*, which had originally entered service in 1719 with 100 guns (reduced to 84 in 1757) and was now a headquarters and accommodation ship. Foley had recommended that he undergo the examination for lieutenant, the first hurdle in every young naval officer's career, as soon as possible. The examining boards, consisting of three senior captains, sat on the first Wednesday of every month and James appeared before that called for January 1800. He was required to produce his journals and certificates of service and answer a series of oral questions on seamanship and navigation. He passed, as he said, in his eighteenth year, the usual age being nineteen, although his commission would not become effective until he was appointed to his next ship. He did not have long to wait; on 27 January he was appointed, probably on Foley's recommendation, as second lieutenant of *Bordelais*, Captain Thomas Manby, which had been recently captured from the French and was fitting out at Hamoaze.

Apart from his duties aboard *Bordelais*, James now had a number of personal matters to attend to. He had to have uniforms made and sit for the portrait requested by Lady Glenbervie as soon as she heard that he had passed the critical examination. He was now approaching the then towering height of six feet three inches and had begun to fill out but he still looked impossibly young for the responsibilities he was about to shoulder, and when he bumped into Captain Whitshed the latter thought so too.[9] Whitshed suggested that he have his hair curled and powdered to make him look a little older, but when this was tried it produced the opposite effect. In the end he had his hair, hitherto worn tied back into a club, cut in the increasingly fashionable short style, which had the desired result. He was now about to embark on the most active and strenuous years of his long career.

NOTES

1. In this respect there is no parallel between the careers of James Gordon and Horatio Hornblower, for the latter never took part in a fleet action. There is nothing surprising in this since, given the Royal Navy's world-wide commitments, only a small percentage of its officers and men were present at any one battle. Furthermore, Forester recognised that, very junior in rank as he was, in any fleet action, the details of which would already be known to anyone with an interest in naval affairs, Hornblower would simply have been a tiny cog in an enormous wheel and unlikely to distinguish himself in any credible way. So although Hornblower's career had also begun in a Seventy-Four, Forester soon transferred him to the more independent and less familiar world of smaller warships, for obvious literary reasons.

2. Both the *Dictionary of National Biography* and a biographical memoir in the *Naval Chronicle* vol. XXXI omit Gordon's service in *Namur* and state that he was in *Goliath* at St Vincent. Gordon's own autobiographical notes make the position quite clear and it seems that he was understandably sensitive regarding his early lack of literacy, which had, of course, resulted in his serving under Whitshed for a second time.

3. It was in this engagement that Nelson lost his right arm. After a brief period of convalescence in England he rejoined St Vincent off Cadiz.

4. The carronade had been introduced into the Royal Navy during the War of American Independence and was then regarded as something of a British secret weapon. It was designed by General Robert Melville and first produced by the Carron Iron Company of Carron, Stirlingshire, hence the name. In essence it was a short, limited-range weapon firing a heavy ball, relying for its effect upon the weight of the projectile rather than, as in the case of long cannon, upon muzzle velocity. Further advantages were that it required a smaller crew to maintain it in action than a cannon of comparable calibre and that its recoil was absorbed by a specially designed 'slide' carriage. Carronades made up the principal armament of many smaller warships and were ideally suited to the Navy's close-engagement tactics; such was the damage they caused that they were nicknamed 'smashers'.

5. In August 1798 some French troops were landed in Ireland to support the rebellion there. They were eventually forced to surrender and a convoy carrying reinforcements was intercepted and destroyed.

6. Egypt was nominally a province of the Turkish Empire but was actually ruled by the Mamelukes, descendants of an élite body of soldier-slaves, who had taken over the country.

7. Naturally the Directory was not unduly worried by his continued absence and waited a full year before sending a fast frigate to bring him home. His troops, having been thus abandoned, fought on until August 1801 when they surrendered to an Anglo–Turkish army and were shipped back to France.

8. Driven inside the fortifications of Valetta by a Maltese uprising and blockaded at sea, the French garrison was starved into surrendering on 5 September 1800. Malta remained a British naval base until after the Second World War.

9. Hornblower at this age was similarly described as gangling.

Chapter 3
LIEUTENANT GORDON

HMS *Bordelais*, though barely a frigate, was more powerfully armed than the conventional sloop, a wide generic term for warships mounting from ten to eighteen guns, and in this she reflected her French ancestry, for in the French service sloops could mount rather more guns than their British counterparts and were known as corvettes.

Once the ship had completed her refit, Captain Manby's first task was to escort a convoy bound for the West Indies. Gordon seems to have settled down very quickly as Second Lieutenant. There were still traces of his youthful wildness, but now they were carefully channelled into demonstrating to his fellow officers and the crew that not only was he up to the job but in many respects could out-perform them. His towering height was matched by commensurate strength, so that he could heave the lead farther than any man aboard, and such was his agility that he could leap in and out of six empty water hogsheads, lined up in succession on the deck, a feat many others attempted without success. Off duty his genial personality came to the fore and he became known as Jem or Jemmy among his peers.

Off the Canary Islands the convoy became scattered by a gale and an enterprising French privateer, *La Mouche*, snapped up two of its stragglers. One was quickly retaken by *Bordelais* but the second, the *Aurora* of London, was seen to be heading for Santa Cruz, Tenerife, under a prize crew. Manby pursued, but the winds were too light to make much headway so throughout 9 January 1801 his crew were hard at work with their sweeps, gradually closing the gap. By the following morning both ships were off Santa Cruz and the enemy was forced to give up within sight of safety.

Little of note took place during the rest of the voyage until, during the last week of January, the convoy began to disperse to its various destinations. Manby had been ordered by Admiral Sir John Duckworth, commanding the West Indies Station, to maintain a position 300 miles east of Barbados to prevent interference from the French islands. At noon on 29 January the wisdom of this became apparent when, at noon, three sails broke the horizon to windward of *Bordelais*. They belonged to a small French squadron, consisting of the brig *La*

Curieuse, with eighteen long 9-pounders and 168 men, commanded by Captain Georges Radelet; a second brig, *La Mutine*, with sixteen long 6-pounders and 156 men, commanded by Captain J. Raybaun; and the schooner *L'Espérance*, six 4-pounders and 52 men, commanded by Captain Haymond. The squadron had been despatched from Cayenne four weeks earlier with the specific object of wreaking havoc among the incoming convoy, but so far its only capture had been a merchant brig, *Susan*, outward bound from Halifax to Surinam, which it had burned. Now, the French bore down on Bordelais and, if they were disappointed to discover that she was not a merchantman, it made little difference as they had her out-gunned and out-manned by almost two-to-one.

This was not an unusual situation for Royal Naval convoy escorts to find themselves in. They always fought back, sometimes against even longer odds than these and often, unexpectedly, they won, proving the old saying that what really counts is not the size of the dog in the fight but the size of the fight in the dog. From the outset, Manby was determined to offer battle and deliberately shortened sail to allow the enemy to come up. As they did so, towards sunset, he wore ship and steered towards them. The French, quite correctly, split his fire by engaging from both sides, but by six o'clock *Bordelais* was running parallel with *La Curieuse* at ten yards' range and, like a terrier, refused to release her prey whichever way she tried to turn. Simultaneously the other enemy vessels were engaging *Bordelais* from the opposite side, but as Manby comments, they 'fought very shy' and, in the French manner, were directing their fire at her rigging in the hope of disabling her. Against *La Curieuse*, *Bordelais'* carronades, reloaded more rapidly and throwing a heavier weight of metal than the former's cannon, were having a fearful effect, smashing into her hull and strewing her decks with dead and wounded. Thirty minutes after the action had begun her guns had been silenced and her consorts, seeing how matters lay, made off. At this, the senior surviving officer aboard *La Curieuse* hailed that she had struck and, her ensign having evidently been shot away, she lowered her topsails.

Manby's first concern was for his own casualties, which were incredibly light, numbering one man killed and seven wounded, including the First Lieutenant, Robert Barrie, who refused to go below, Master's Mate Mr J. Jones and Midshipman J. Lions. What happened after *Bordelais* had launched her boats to take possession of the prize is recounted by Manby himself:

'The killed and wounded in the Corvette amounted to near fifty; her deck, fore and aft, being covered with the dying and the dead. The French

THE CARIBBEAN
THEATRE OF WAR

BAHAMAS

CAICOS

TURKS ISLANDS

CUBA

HISPANIOLA

CAPE SAMANA

VIRGIN
ISLANDS

SANTIAGO
DE CUBA

LÉOGANE · Fr | Sp

JAMAICA

AGUADILLA

BARBUDA
St KITTS
ANTIGUA

PORT SALUT

PORT
ROYAL

San Domingo · PUERTO RICO

SAINT
DOMINGUE
(HAITI)

SAN
DOMINGO

GUADALOUPE

DOMINICA

MARTINIQUE

St LUCIA

LESSER ANTILLES

DIAMOND ROCK

St VINCENT

BARBADOS

CARIBBEAN SEA

CURACAO

BONAIRE

GRENADA

TOBAGO

MARGARITA

CARACAS

TRINIDAD

CARTHAGENA

GUYANA

Captain survived but a few hours, having lost both his legs, and many of the prisoners were in an equally pitiable state. This Capture, which, after being more than an hour in our possession, was found to be rapidly sinking, in consequence of her innumerable shot holes. Every exertion was made to preserve her; but, alas! at eight she foundered close beside us. I had, some time previous to this event, ordered everybody to quit her; but British humanity, while striving to extricate the wounded Frenchmen from destruction, weighed so forcibly with Mr Archibald Montgomery and twenty brave fellows, that they persevered in this meritorious service until the vessel sank under them. The floating wreck, I rejoice to say, buoyed up many from destruction, but with sorrow I mention Mr Frederick Spence and Mr Auckland, two promising young gentlemen, with five of my gallant crew, unfortunately perished. The delay occasioned by this unhappy event, securing 120 prisoners, knotting the rigging, and repairing sails, detained me until eleven before I could pursue the flying enemy, which I assure you, was done with all alacrity, but without success, as night favoured their escape; but I think I can safely aver they are sufficiently damaged to spoil their cruise.'

Manby's report to Admiral Duckworth was written three days later while *Bordelais* was lying at anchor in Carlisle Bay, Barbados. 'I cannot conclude this account of my proceedings without informing you how highly I approve the conduct of Lieutenant Robert Barrie, Lieutenant James Alexander Gordon, Mr McCleverty, the Master, and Mr Montgomery, my acting Lieutenant.[1] The proceedings of Warrant and Petty Officers gave me every satisfaction; and I have not words to offer sufficiently in the praise of the Ship's Company for their steady obedience to my orders in not wasting a single shot.'

This was the first occasion on which Gordon's name was favourably drawn to the attention of his superiors and marked the beginning of the reputation which he would make for himself in the West Indies during the next few years. This area, particularly the Caribbean Sea, bounded to the north by the large islands of the Greater Antilles (Cuba, Jamaica, Hispaniola and Puerto Rico), to the east by the island chains of the Lesser Antilles (Leeward and Windward Islands), and to the south and west by South and Central America, was one of immense economic and strategic importance to all the contending powers. The agriculture of the islands produced all manner of profitable goods, including cotton, indigo, tobacco, ginger, spices, cocoa, coffee, molasses, rum and, most important of all, sugar. Annually, they produced vast sums to boost the economies of the nations that owned them. Some measure of their value can be gauged from the fact that during the negotiations leading up the Treaty of Paris, which ended the Seven Years War in 1763, the French indicated their willingness to abandon any claim to their lost holdings in Canada provided that the islands of Martinique and Guadaloupe were returned to them. Indeed, throughout the wars of the eighteenth century, possession of the islands was a constant bone of contention between the warring powers, the evidence of which remains to this day in the form of powerful fortresses, some still in use, others derelict and overgrown, protecting every harbour and anchorage of note. Naturally, with so many valuable cargoes plying the Caribbean, the area acted as a magnet for pirates, who found innumerable bolt-holes among the myriad small islands and keys. When not officially at war, the Royal Navy was constantly hunting them down, so that the West Indies Station was always very active. During time of war the pirates added an air of legitimacy to their activities by becoming privateers.[2]

There was, however, a much darker side to life in the West Indies. Tropical diseases, of which yellow fever was the most virulent, claimed the lives of so many Europeans that British regiments stationed there regarded it as a death sentence; the Royal Navy suffered too, but not to the same extent, since life afloat was healthier than ashore. This meant that manual work of the plantations could only be carried out by the dwindling population of indigenous natives or by slave labour imported from Africa. The United Kingdom was on the point of banning the infamous slave trade, but slavery in the islands would continue to exist for some years to come and the prospect of a slave rising was something that local naval and military commanders always had to bear in mind.

The French Revolution had introduced a further element into the already complex strategic considerations of the Caribbean, the flashpoint being the island of Hispaniola, one third of which was owned by France under the name of Saint Domingue, the rest being owned by Spain and named Santo Domingo. In Saint Domingue, or Haiti as it became known, violent power struggles broke out between royalists and republicans and whites and mulattos. The slaves, more cruelly used than perhaps anywhere else in the Caribbean, having learned that the Revolution was based on the principles of Liberty, Equality and Fraternity, rose *en masse* in 1791 and, having slaughtered many of their former masters, carried the rising across the border into Santo Domingo. The British, already involved in the neutralisation or capture of French and Spanish possessions, were deeply concerned that the rising should not spread to Jamaica and elsewhere. A British expedition was mounted to Hispaniola to contain the threat, which it did successfully at a heavy cost in yellow fever victims, but it was not until 1800 that order was fully restored by a former Haitian slave, Pierre Dominique Toussaint L'Ouverture, a man of honour and real ability. The Peace of Amiens (1802) saw the islands of Martinique and Guadaloupe again restored to the French, who quickly re-established slavery. Naturally this caused serious alarm among the former slaves in Haiti, who had established an uneasy *modus vivendi* with the whites and mulattos. Although Toussaint was under immense pressure to sever the connection with France, he doubted the wisdom of this. But balancing the volatile factions within Haiti was a dangerous game and, for the sake of form, the French commissioners were sent home. The idea of a French possession being ruled in a semi-autonomous manner by a former slave was not all to Bonaparte's liking and he dispatched his brother-in-law, General Victor Leclerc, with 25,000 troops to restore French authority.

Such was the volatile situation in the Caribbean when *Bordelais* left Barbados for Jamaica, having called briefly at Martinique en route. At Jamaica she came under the command of Rear-Admiral Lord Seymour and spent some time repairing her damage before being sent to cruise off Cape Samana, Santo Domingo, covering the Mona Passage between Hispaniola and Puerto Rico, which was still in Spanish hands.[3] Here considerable damage was done to the enemy's local shipping, a period of which Gordon recalled, with a frustrating lack of detail: 'I was almost constantly away in the boats and took and destroyed a great number of vessels. I had the command of the boats of *Bordelais* and of — , I forget the name of the ship, in an attack made upon vessels in Aguado (Aguadilla) Bay, in the island of Puerto Rico, when several men were killed and wounded in the other ship's boats.'

Evidently, this particular cutting-out expedition was successful, for he goes on to say that one of the prizes taken was fitted out and manned as a tender.[4] Gordon wanted command of the tender and pestered Manby about it, but the latter declined and appointed his acting-Lieutenant, Montgomery. Had he granted Gordon's wish there would be no tale to tell, for the tender was lost with all hands shortly after.

Manby decided to return to Aguadilla with the object of taking a French schooner lying there. This time, however, the Spanish defences were much stronger and there was a furious exchange of fire with the shore batteries. 'Without losing a man', commented Gordon, 'we were so much cut up in our masts and rigging that we were obliged to bear up to Port Royal for refitting and a new foremast.'

The refit completed, Manby returned to his cruising station. A small sloop laden with wood was cut out of a minor harbour on the Puerto Rican coast. After she had been cleared and fitted as a tender, Gordon was given command with seven men and two boys as crew. The pleasure of having his first command, however, was to be short-lived, for at this point, in the autumn of 1801, his fortunes underwent a sudden and dramatic change for the worse.

'A few days after sailing,' he wrote, 'I was chased and taken by a French privateer with one gun and 60 men. I was carried into Port Lake or Salu, a small bay to the west of Auxlayes, St Domingue, with a sloop laden with salt, a prize of the *Bordelais*, which had only left the ship the night before; she had a midshipman and four men on board. The midshipman, Mr Mathewson, spoke French very well, which was a great comfort to me, as I did not understand the language. The captain of the privateer gave us in charge of the commandant of the place, a captain in the (French) service, who gave us a good supper, bed and breakfast, and was particularly kind. He told us we must march to Auxlayes. I said I could not walk and that Mr Mathewson and myself ought to have horses furnished us. After a great deal of disputing we were mounted upon two country horses, but before we had gone three miles, we wished we had not had horses, for the stirrups broke, and having no other clothes than a round jacket and a pair of jean trousers, I was soon unable to walk.[5] I forget the distance to Auxlayes, but the country was beautiful.

'On arrival we were taken before the Governor, General La Plume, a negro but a good, kind creature who was very attentive to us always. The seamen were sent to prison and we were put on parole. An Italian, Mr Nathan, took me to his house and Mathewson went to the house of a Mr Cunningham. All the American merchants were very hospitable and attentive to us. I saw several reviews of black troops; the men were very fine fellows. I found no difficulty in getting money for my bills [of exchange], and as my people were not well fed I expended nearly £30 for them, but never having taken any voucher I was not able to be repaid, and in consequence of the great changes that subsequently took place in the island, it was impossible to get any vouchers.'

These changes referred to by Gordon stemmed from the determined resistance offered by Toussaint's troops to Leclerc's French expeditionary force. Among the Haitians at least anti-French feelings ran high, to the extent that the crew of the privateer which had captured Gordon were themselves thrown into prison.[6] The British, on the other hand, found themselves enjoying something close to popularity, to the extent that the only white men permitted to move around Auxlayes after dark were Gordon and Mathewson.

Gordon's experience as a prisoner of war can hardly be described as harsh and it lasted barely four months, at the end of which General La Plume dispatched him and his crew to Jamaica on *cartel* (i.e., written agreement concerning the exchange of prisoners) under the command of Captain Kelpoisson, the Captain of the Port of Auxlayes and one of very white men allowed any authority there.

'On the guard-boat boarding us, going into Port Royal, the officer told us that peace was proclaimed.[7] This so delighted poor Kelpoisson that he took the astonished lieutenant round the neck and kissed him! I was in a jacket and trousers and, dressed as I was, I was taken on board the *Sans Pareille* with Mathewson and ten men, one having died. The First Lieutenant did not remember me and after a number of questions he said I would make a very good fore-topman. I at last made myself known and, the *Bordelais* being in port, I went on board and got to the mess table before any of my old messmates knew, as there was not a person on board.'

Shortly after Gordon's return, Captain Manby handed over command to Captain John Hayes and *Bordelais* was ordered home, being paid off at Chatham.

NOTES

1. Acting lieutenants were either midshipmen or masters' mates awaiting the opportunity to sit the promotion examination. Their rank applied only aboard the ship in which they were serving.

2. Anyone could fit out a ship and become a privateer, provided his stated intention was to prey upon his country's enemies. In the United Kingdom a privateer's licence could be obtained from the Post Office. A few privateers became rich beyond their wildest dreams, but the risk of sudden death or capture were proportionately high.

3. Cape Samana was also the scene of one of Lieutenant Hornblower's most remarkable exploits. Several privateers had taken refuge in the upper reaches of Samana Bay, where Hornblower's ship, *Renown*, could not follow because of her draught. Hornblower solved the problem by having a 9-pounder cannon, carriage and ammunition hauled up the seaward face of a headland from a launch below. The gun was then manhandled across the headland and engaged the enemy with red hot shot until they surrendered.

   Forester's inspiration for this incident was provided by the Diamond Rock affair. In 1804 the British blockade of the heavily fortified harbour of Fort de France, Martinique, was being frustrated by enemy vessels creeping through the passage between the south coast of the island and Diamond Rock. This feature has been compared to the Bass Rock and resembles a gigantic tooth towering out of the sea with sheer cliffs rising straight from the water's edge on the southern or seaward side. The northern side of the rock is also extremely steep and covered with vegetation but is not so precipitous. Captain Murray Maxwell of the *Centaur* believed that if a battery of guns could be established on top of the rock access to the channel would be denied to the French. A line, followed by a stream cable, was carried to the summit from *Centaur*, anchored close inshore to seaward, and secured. A traveller, i.e., a pulley block was attached to the cable and a 24-pounder gun suspended from it. Using tackles those on the summit hauled the gun upwards, its passage being steadied by lines to boats below. In this way, more guns, carriages, shot, powder, water and rations for three officers and 120 men were hoisted up the rock. As soon as these had been emplaced, any French vessel attempting to use the channel was in serious danger of being blown apart. The Admiralty was so impressed by this display of initiative on the part of Murray Maxwell, of whom much more anon, that the rock was granted the status of a sloop and was entered on the records as HMS Diamond Rock.

4. The problem with sloops and slightly larger warships like Bordelais was that the amount of time they could spend on station was restricted by their own limited supplies of fresh water and food. Sometimes they could replenish from a larger warship, but acquiring a tender with which they could rendezvous at intervals provided a better solution. The tender would make regular runs to the parent vessel's home port, in this case Port Royal, bringing back fresh water, victuals, mail and returning prize crews.

5. Hornblower, it may be recalled, had a similar unpleasant experience in the short story 'The Bewildered Pirates' (Hornblower in the West Indies).

6. The troubled state of Haitian politics created a dangerous scenario in which Forester could have placed Hornblower, with interesting results. Certainly there is a gap in Hornblower's

recorded exploits between 14 November 1800 and 27 June 1801. In *The Life and Times of Horatio Hornblower*, C. Northcote Parkinson makes the point that when Hornblower visited Haiti in 1822, while commanding the West Indies Station, he referred in passing to an earlier and fairly dramatic visit, without going into detail. Forester's intention may have been to return to this period, possibly with a short story inspired by Gordon's experiences as a prisoner of war. Very probably the source was the biography of Gordon found in Volume 31 of the *Naval Chronicle*, which tells us that Gordon: '... being in charge of a prize, was obliged by stress of bad weather to put into a port of the island of St Domingo; where, for some cause of offence which we have not heard explained, he was refused his parole, and imprisoned by Toussaint; from whose power he was not recovered without much trouble and correspondence on the part of the Admiral [Sir John Duckworth] then commanding the fleet on the Jamaica Station. During his detention he suffered considerable hardships; and it was a long time before he entirely recovered from the effects of the treatment which he had so unjustly experienced.' As we know from Gordon's own narrative, most of this is wildly inaccurate, although it contains the basis of a good story. Any correspondence between Duckworth and Toussaint would relate to the legality of the latter holding prisoners on behalf of the French.

7. During the short-lived Peace of Amiens (27 March 1802–16 May 1803) the Royal Navy paid off hundreds of ships as they returned home, putting most of their officers on half pay. See *Lieutenant Hornblower*.

Chapter 4
FIRST COMMAND

G ordon spent some time ashore with the Glenbervies but soon received a new appointment as Second Lieutenant of the brig *Racoon*, armed with sixteen 18-pounder carronades and two long 6-pounder chasers, recently recommissioned under Captain Wilson Rathbone at Portsmouth. *Racoon* sailed for the West Indies in August 1802 and, on arriving at Port Royal, Captain Rathbone was posted to another ship. The brig's First Lieutenant, Austin Bissell, was promoted commander in his place and Gordon was moved up the ladder to become First Lieutenant.

At about this time he received a last, sad letter from his Grandfather Mercer, whose own failing health had never recovered from the loss of his wife in January.

> 'My Dear Jamie – I find that you are again to set out for the West Indies, of which I highly approve, for at your time of life, promotion ought to be your object, and I pray that God's good Providence, which has hitherto been manifest in your favour, may accompany you through life, and that you may be happy and successful in all your undertakings, and by your conduct deserve to be so ... In your early infancy you contributed much to my enjoyment, and to the enjoyment of the dear companion then alive. Be assured, my dear Jamie, that you are very dear to me indeed.
> Farewell, and God be with you.'

Major Mercer lingered on for a further year, leaving Gordon half his small property at Achnancant. He would, before he died, be gladdened by news that his favourite grandson had gone far towards fulfilling his wishes.

Racoon's first task was to proceed into the Gulf of Honduras where, Gordon relates, Bissell 'was actively employed in settling disputes between the Spanish Guardacostas at Truxillo (Trujillo) and our merchant vessels.' This was fairly routine peacetime business for the Royal Navy in the Caribbean, where the Spaniards disliked other nations trading with their colonies and were inclined to create local difficulties. Usually a display of official firmness, backed by the presence of a warship, was enough to resolve the problem and, though Gordon does not go into detail, this seems to have sufficed, for *Racoon* was soon back in Port Royal and undergoing a refit.

Very few people believed that the United Kingdom and Napoleon Bonaparte, who had recently had himself proclaimed Consul for Life, could co-exist peacefully for long. With this in mind, when *Racoon*'s refit was complete she was sent to cruise the north coast of Jamaica and impress all the seamen that could be found in the ports there. The war broke out again on 16 May 1803, and when *Racoon* returned to Port Royal the 120 men she had picked up were transferred to HMS *Theseus*.

Strategic considerations in the West Indies still centred on the Island of Hispaniola where the French under Leclerc had become embroiled in a savage guerrilla war against Toussaint's troops. In June 1802 Leclerc, whose army was being wasted by disease, had offered an amnesty and Toussaint, anxious to end a decade of strife, agreed to negotiate. He was treacherously seized and sent to France, where he died in prison the following year. Hostilities were resumed, the Haitians now being commanded by Jean Jacques Dessalines who, like Toussaint, was a strong and able leader, albeit one with burning personal ambitions and a strong streak of cruelty. Leclerc himself succumbed to yellow fever, and his troops, losing ground, sick and demoralised, began leaving the island during the latter half of 1803. Dessalines wasted no time in having himself crowned as Emperor Alexandre I and ordering a massacre of all the remaining whites.

It was against this background that *Racoon* was ordered to cruise off Hispaniola in July 1803. She was a lucky ship and since her original commissioning in 1795 had taken no fewer than nine French privateers. As might be expected in the circumstances, and indeed as Gordon relates, there was plenty for her to do. 'On 6th July, on rounding Cape Rosa, we observed a schooner at anchor, protected by a battery, which we attacked. I was ordered away in a boat to bring her out, but after having one man killed and three wounded, I was obliged to return to the brig. We sank the schooner. On the 7th we took the schooner *La Vertu*, mounting two guns, with troops on board, and destroyed several other small vessels. On the 8th we took the sloop *L'Ami du Celonnot*, of two guns, and had a smart cannonade with a battery on shore. On the 9th we chased a schooner on shore in Bernadier Bay and knocked her to pieces with one gun.'

On the morning of 11 July *Racoon* was cruising between the island of Guamaba and the southern peninsula of Haiti when a French warship of similar size was observed lying at anchor in the port of Leogane, some eighteen miles west of Port au Prince. She was the corvette *Le Lodi*, originally pierced for twenty guns but now, perhaps because of the deteriorating situation ashore, reduced to ten 6-pounder cannon and 61 men. Bissell, of course, could not have known this and probably expected a stiff fight as *Racoon* bore down on her, especially as the French could be seen putting springs on their cables in preparation. Although there is no record to that effect, it seems probable that *Lodi* opened fire first because *Racoon*'s sails and rigging were subsequently reported as being a good deal cut about, and this was unlikely to have happened when the ships came to close quarters. At 1445 hours *Racoon* dropped anchor within thirty yards of her opponent and, at Bissell's direction, a spring was put on her own cable.[1] As First Lieutenant, supervision of this task, carried out under fire and within easy musket shot, would have been Gordon's responsibility. For thirty minutes the two ships hammered away at each other. By the end of that period *Racoon*'s heavier weight of metal had caused serious damage to her opponent, one quarter of whose crew were down. *Lodi*'s commander, Lieutenant Pierre-Isaac Taupier, cut his cables, almost certainly with the idea of running the ship aground to prevent capture rather than escape. Bissell did likewise and, as *Lodi* was all but unrigged, quickly forereached the Frenchman. After the fight had continued for a further ten minutes, Taupier struck his colours and called across that he had surrendered.

Bissell's dispatch to Admiral Duckworth, dated '16th July 1803, off the East End of Jamaica', was clearly sent in to Kingston by tender and suggests that *Racoon*'s return to her home port was being delayed by the need to escort the jury-rigged *Lodi*. 'I am happy to say that I had not a man killed,' wrote Bissell. 'And the only person wounded is Mr Thomas Gill, Master's Mate, whose left arm was carried away by a shot; a very promising young man, who has served his time in the Navy and will, if he survives, do credit to your patronage. The loss of the enemy is one killed and thirteen or fourteen wounded, by their account. The conduct of Mr James Alexander Gordon, the First Lieutenant, on this as well as many other recent occasions, has been highly exemplary and praiseworthy; and I have much pleasure in informing you that the whole of the Officers and Ship's Company behaved fully to my satisfaction.' Bissell appended a list of his depredations off Haiti since 5 July and in due course Duckworth passed on the dispatch to Sir Evan Nepean, First Secretary of the Admiralty Board, who authorised its publication in the *London Gazette*.

This was not the first time that Gordon's name had appeared in the *Gazette* but it was the first occasion on which he had been so singled out.[2] He received numerous letters from delighted relatives, of which the most important was that from Lord Glenbervie.

'My Dear James – As soon as I saw your captain's letter, with his account of the taking of the *Lodi*, and read of the warm praises bestow'd on you in it, I wrote both to Lord St Vincent and Captain Markham of the Admiralty, and by the answer I received, I find the First Lord entertains no doubt that Sir John Duckworth has promoted you before now. It would be difficult to express the joy of your aunt, Maria and myself, when we read Captain Bissell's dispatch. I am persuaded he is a gallant officer and a kind-hearted, worthy fellow, and I know, from other circumstances, that he has a great friendship for you. We trust before this time next year that circumstances may bring you to this country, and your aunt begins to anticipate the pleasure of a party to visit her nephew, Captain Gordon, on board his own ship. For all family news I refer you to your sister. Your poor grandfather's health is in a most uncomfortable state. We are in daily expectation of letters from you with your own account of your own Battle of *Lodi*.'

As indicated, Lord Glenbervie's influence at the Admiralty was not necessary to secure his nephew's promotion since Duckworth had, indeed, already made up his mind on the subject, this being specifically referred to in a contemporary letter from Lady Glenbervie to Gordon: 'I flatter myself that you will inform us of your promotion, as Admiral Duckworth has written to your uncle that it shall take place as soon as he can manage it, consistent with his other engagements.'

Having repaired her damage in Montego Bay, *Racoon* was next ordered to cruise off Cuba, whither the French were fleeing from Haiti. During the course of one morning she fell in with five French privateers, one of which was captured and one run on shore and destroyed before the rest escaped. Gordon was given command of the prize, which was manned as a tender, and after several more vessels had been captured he was sent on ship's business into Santiago de Cuba. On 17 August, while he was away, Bissell met, fought and destroyed the French naval brig *La Mutine*. Some sources claim that Gordon was present during this engagement, but his own papers make it clear that he was not; had he been, he would have been able to confirm whether the French ship was the same vessel against which he had fought when in *Bordelais*, the chance of which seems likely.

When Gordon rejoined *Racoon* the brig and her prizes sailed for Port Royal. There he went down with a bout of yellow fever and *Racoon* sailed on her next cruise without him. He seems to have been ill for several weeks but his strong constitution and good nursing by friends ashore enabled him to pull through. On 22 October Sir John Duckworth sent for him.

'He told me he would put me in as captain of one of the French man-of-war's brig prizes then in port, as Lodi was found to be unfit for service. At that moment, the *Racoon* made her pennant and Sir John told me that he would Post Captain Bissell, and make me commander of the *Racoon*.[3] I commissioned her, and sailed next morning, 23rd October 1803, for the north of Jamaica. I was employed here for some time. We took one schooner with troops and disarmed a great number of soldiers who were flying from St Domingo in an American merchant brig. After refitting at Port Royal, I was sent to Nassau, New Providence, Bahamas, then threatened with an attack by the French troops at Cuba who had escaped from St Domingo. On 16 March 1804 I captured a National [French naval] transport, *L'Argo*, mounting six guns, commanded by *Enseigne de Vaisseau* Dupurie, with 50 men and 20 officers and seamen, from New Orleans, bound for France. On 5th April I captured the privateer *L'Aventure*, mounting one gun and two swivels with 28 men.'

And so his career of destruction among the enemy's shipping continued throughout the year, his prizes including the privateers *L'Alliance* and *L'Asienne*, respectively armed with six and eight guns and manned with appropriately large crews, and an American schooner laden with coffee.[4]

Gordon now found himself on the fringe of great events, although he was unaware of the fact at the time. In December 1804 Spain once again declared war on the United Kingdom. Napoleon, now Emperor of the French, had for some time been assembling his Grande Armée at Boulogne with an idea of invading England and only his inability to secure control of the Channel had prevented his doing so. He now instituted a complex scheme intended to draw away a major portion of British naval strength. Implementation of this was delayed but on 25 March 1805 Vice-Admiral Pierre Villeneuve broke out of Toulon with eleven ships, seven frigates, two brigs and a number of troop transports. Having caught Nelson wrong-footed, he passed through the Straits of Gibraltar and was joined by three Spanish ships off Cadiz. He then headed out into the Atlantic and reached Martinique on 14 May, where he was joined by more Spanish vessels, which increased the strength of his fleet to eighteen ships of the line, seven frigates and four corvettes. In the West Indies the French troops were, in addition to other tasks, to reinforce the remaining garrisons in Haiti and San Domingo. The next phase of Napoleon's plan involved Villeneuve's re-crossing the Atlantic and breaking the blockades of Ferrol and Rochefort. These events, coupled with the landing of no less than 18,000 troops in Ireland, would, he reasoned, distract the British and cause them to disperse their strength, enabling Admiral Honor Ganteaume to break out of Brest with his 21 ships of the line. When Ganteaume was joined by Villeneuve the combined French and Spanish fleet in the Channel would number some 40 ships of the line, a force considered quite capable of protecting the Grande Armée during its short passage to England. The plan, conceived by a man with no understanding of naval matters, was over-complicated and absurdly ambitious. In fact, Nelson was already in hot pursuit of Villeneuve and, after various twists and turns in the story, the long chase was to end with the destruction of the latter's combined fleet at Trafalgar on 21 October.

It was, in fact, Gordon who provided the first warning to those in Jamaica that something was afoot. During the early days of May 1805 *Racoon* was patrolling off the port of Santo Domingo when the French hove in sight. Taking care to avoid contact, Gordon shadowed them until they dropped anchor in the harbour and then, well aware of possible implications, set all sail for Port Royal. Duckworth took a very serious view of the situation and immediately informed the Governor, who in turn summoned the island's Council. Gordon was closely questioned by everyone about the enemy's strength, and as an attack on Jamaica was a distinct possibility, martial law was proclaimed. In due course it became apparent that no threat had existed, but the report did add a piece to the intelligence jigsaw that would ultimately reveal French intentions. Gordon's reminiscences on the subject are modest to the point of being dismissive, but Duckworth clearly thought otherwise. *Racoon*'s young commander was promptly promoted to Post-Captain and given a larger command.[5]

NOTES

1. James's *Naval History, 1886* edition, vol. 3, p. 188, says that the action commenced at '3h.15m P.M.'. Bissell's dispatch, however, gives the time as 'a Quarter before Three (PM)', so providing one example of several older English usages still common in the United States. This form had evidently fallen into disuse by the time William James was writing, hence the minor error.

2. It had, along with others, appeared in Captain Manby's account of *Bordelais*' action against three French privateers, which had also been printed in the *Gazette*.

3. In January 1807 Captain Bissell was commanding the 90-gun *Blenheim* when she vanished without trace off the coast of Madagascar. Among those aboard was Admiral Sir Thomas Troubridge, one of Nelson's original 'band of brothers'.

4. Naturally the Americans objected to having their shipping interfered with in this way, but accepted that merchants who chose to trade in a blockaded war zone did so at their own risk. What they did not accept was the impressment of seamen from American vessels for service in

the Royal Navy. Officially, such impressments involved British subjects only, but the rules were regularly broken. The practice was a major contributory factor in the causes of the War of 1812.

5. This would have been an ideal occasion for Horatio Hornblower to have distinguished himself. But his adventures in *Hotspur* and *Atropos* found him employed elsewhere and Forester filled the awkward gap with *Hornblower and the Crisis*, in which his hero is tasked with delivering forged orders from Bonaparte to Villeneuve, instructing the latter to leave harbour and give battle, contrary to his better judgement. Sadly, Forester died before completing the story, although we know that he intended the mission to succeed and that the result would be Trafalgar.

Chapter 5
OFF ROTA, 4 APRIL 1808

On 16 May 1805 Gordon was appointed commander of the 28-gun frigate *Laegera*, formerly the Spanish *Diligentia*. It was, no doubt, with very mixed feelings that he left the companionable little *Racoon* in which he had served for almost three years, but at this stage of his career command of even an elderly Sixth Rate was a most welcome step on the ladder of promotion.

His first task was to escort a convoy home from the West Indies, which he accomplished without incident, and shortly after arriving he was delighted to learn that his name had been added to the list of Post-Captains, a most remarkable achievement for a 23-year-old. However, at this stage his health once again broke down completely, the after effects of two bouts of yellow fever being complicated by a respiratory infection. For a while he lay seriously ill in a Portsmouth inn, being bled regularly between fainting fits. This was an especially cruel twist of Fate, for he was compelled to resign command of the *Laegera* and join the ranks of other junior Post-Captains awaiting their next command on half pay.

Somehow, he survived both the illness and its supposed cure. As soon as he was fit enough to travel he joined his father, who was now Paymaster Western District and living in Marlborough with James's half-sister Frances and his two younger sisters. Nearby lived Mr John Ward, 'a solicitor and a man of property who was the principal person in the town, and universally esteemed and respected'. John Ward had three daughters, Eliza, Margaret and Lydia, who were close friends of Frances's and daily visitors to the Gordon household. Thus James found himself being thoroughly spoiled by young ladies and being drawn into their social activities. This was exactly the sort of situation so well known to and so immortalised by Jane Austen. Although Eliza and Margaret were the most lively of the Ward sisters, it was the reserved Lydia, then in her 19th year, that James fell for, and she returned his affection. Seeing how matters stood, both his father and Mr Ward were happy to allow the relationship to continue but were opposed to placing it on a formal footing because of James's dependence on his profession and the inevitability of his return to active service. James and Lydia accepted the position but a clear understanding existed between them and when, eventually, he returned to sea, he took a lock of her hair with him. During his enforced spell of idleness he also journeyed north to Aberdeen, where relatives and old family friends would have been startled, and not a little impressed, to learn that the handsome young captain with prize money in his pocket was the same wild boy who had been sent out into the world so long ago. In the aftermath of Trafalgar it was good to be a naval officer on leave, although Gordon must have felt bitterly disappointed that he had missed the climactic battle of the naval war with France and Spain.

The remainder of 1805 passed without prospect of a command, as did the whole of 1806. Anxiously Gordon watched his funds begin to dwindle and one is reminded of a similar period in Horatio Hornblower's career, during which Forester's hero first served unofficially aboard a Revenue cutter and was then engaged as a professional cards player by the proprietor of the Long Rooms in Portsmouth. There is no suggestion that Gordon was ever forced to resort to such measures, but many half-pay officers were, particularly those with dependents.

It was not until 18 June 1807 that Gordon received his next appointment, which placed him almost exactly where he had been before his illness. His new command was another Sixth Rate, the *Mercury* (28), a Thames-built frigate which had been launched as long ago as 1779, when the War of American Independence was at its height, and was now nearing the end of her useful life. Nonetheless Gordon was happy enough to have her and to get back to sea.

Mercury and smaller ships like her were the Navy's maids-of-all-work. For a short period under Gordon she was employed on convoy escort duty, initially to Newfoundland and then to the embattled island of Jersey, which lay within easy reach of the French coast, girdled by Martello towers and other coastal fortifications constantly manned by the island's militia. At Jersey Gordon received orders to join the fleet that was blockading Cadiz.

This fine natural harbour, off which, of course, he had performed blockade duty ten years earlier, is protected from the Atlantic swell and the prevailing wind by a long, thin-waisted peninsula running south–north. The city of Cadiz lies in a virtually impregnable huddle at the northern end of this, the seaward approach being covered by the Castillo de San Sebastián. Immediately opposite, on the northern shore of Cadiz Bay, lies the small town of Rota, protected during the Napoleonic Wars by a battery constructed on the adjacent headland.

In the aftermath of Trafalgar eleven line-of-battle ships belonging to Villeneuve's Franco–Spanish Combined Fleet had staggered in succession into Cadiz through one of the most notorious gales in history. Since then these battle-torn survivors had moved hardly at all and the jest was that they were in danger of grounding on their own rubbish. Even worse, the morale of their crews had declined steadily in the two-and-a-half years that they had lain at anchor, and with it their efficiency. This, inevitably, was the fate of any blockaded fleet-in-being, while its captors maintained their edge of efficiency simply because they were constantly at sea and therefore able to hone their techniques in gunnery and seamanship to their hearts' content.

The French and Spanish admirals were fully aware that if they did not get their ships back to sea they would simply rot, literally and morally. The principal problem was that before a break-out could even be considered, the extensive damage sustained at Trafalgar and during the subsequent storm would have to be repaired. For this, large quantities of ships' timber, spars and cordage would be required, far more than could be assembled in a reasonably short space of time using the primitive road system of the Iberian peninsula. In the normal course of events, moreover, such stores would reach Cadiz by sea, but the daily presence of the British frigates, brigs and sloops inshore, and the Seventy-Fours and larger vessels hugging the horizon, apparently doomed any such attempt before it could begin.

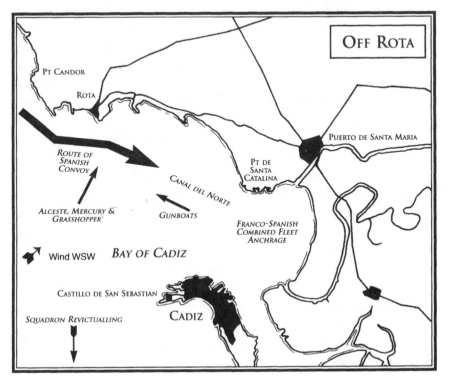

On the other hand, as some resourceful Spanish officer must have pointed out, if a convoy of tartanes was employed, the chances of success would be greatly enhanced. The tartane was a Spanish coaster in which the typical Mediterranean features of a high stem and a lateen mainsail were combined with a northern European bowsprit and jib. It was fast, especially when running down-wind, and drew little water even when fully laden. Taking advantage of the shallows along the northern shore of the bay to slip past the bigger British ships, a convoy should experience little difficulty in breaking through into Cadiz harbour.

No one expected the British to allow a convoy free passage on these grounds alone, and every consideration had been given to its protection. The immediate escort would consist of twenty gunboats each of which mounted at least one heavy gun and could be propelled either by sails or sweeps. In shallow water or windless conditions, therefore, these craft had a marked advantage, since they could lie off the vulnerable quarters of conventional warships and slowly batter them to pieces.

In addition, full advantage was taken of the fact that during the last few miles of the convoy's route a road ran beside the shore, and several batteries of horse artillery were detailed to keep pace with the ships along this and open fire on their account if the occasion demanded. This seems to have been the optimistic addition of a soldier, for in naval terms the field-piece was a mere pop-gun, and not even a full battery could hope to compete with the weight of metal thrown by a small brig. The heavier weapons mounted in the coastal defence battery at Rota were, of course, a very different matter, and a convoy's final entry into the harbour would be covered by a simultaneous sortie of yet more gunboats from Cadiz itself.

Careful observation told the Spaniards that the strength of the blockade varied as ships arrived and departed in the cycle of re-victualling, and it remained only to choose a suitable moment when it was at its weakest. During the first week of April 1808 that moment seemed to have arrived. The telescopes sweeping the sea from the ramparts of the Castillo de San Sebastián revealed no trace of the larger warships. This in itself meant nothing, for they were often below the horizon or concealed from watchers on shore by poor visibility; what confirmed their departure was the absence of signal flags soaring up the hoists of the inshore vessels. Cadiz was, for the moment, blockaded by two frigates and a brig. Quickly the news was passed northward along the coast to the waiting convoy.

Commanding the squadron off Cadiz was Rear-Admiral Purvis, flying his flag in *Atlas*. Provisions aboard his ships were low and when five victuallers joined he called in his major units to complete as quickly as possible, leaving the frigate *Alceste* (38), commanded by Captain Murray Maxwell, on station three miles north-west of San Sebastián lighthouse, reinforcing her with Gordon's *Mercury* and the brig *Grasshopper* (18), commanded by Lieutenant Thomas Searle. Purvis obviously had no idea of the enemy's intentions or he would never have left so light a covering force; as it was, he felt uneasy enough to order Captain Sir John Gore in *Revenge*, followed by *Excellent*, to return as soon as they had revictualled.

Monday 4 April dawned fine with a light off-shore breeze and a slight haze. As the morning advanced the warmth of the spring sun began to make itself felt. *Alceste*, *Mercury* and *Grasshopper* turned slowly about their anchors in the mouth of Cadiz Bay, and there was nothing to suggest that this day would be any different from hundreds of others in the apparently endless blockade. Just out of range lay the fortress of San Sebastián with the scarlet and gold standard of Spain floating from its flagstaff. Beyond were the walls of Cadiz, embracing the domes of the cathedral and other churches. Behind the city lay the harbour, in which could be seen the incomplete masts and spars of the French and Spanish warships. On the opposite shore a clutter of white walls and red-tiled roofs marked Rota, fronted by a line of shallows over which the sea pushed lazily to break on a rocky coastline stretching north-west to Punta Candor and beyond. Inland lay an uninteresting landscape of marshland and saltpan through which tortuous streams wound their turgid course to the sea.

Noon came and went. The two sides continued to observe each other, the Spaniards with a growing sense of anticipation. Then, a little before 3 o'clock, the lateen sails of the convoy appeared off Punta Candor, having rounded which the tartanes and their escort headed straight into Cadiz Bay, achieving complete tactical surprise over the British squadron. The subsequent engagement was described by Murray Maxwell, the senior captain, in his dispatch to Admiral Purvis, who forwarded it to Lord Collingwood.

'His Majesty's Ship *Alceste*, in-shore,
off Cadiz, April 4, 1808

Sir,

I have the honour to inform you, that when at anchor today with His Majesty's ship *Mercury*, and *Grasshopper*, brig, St Sebastián's lighthouse SE distant three miles, wind WSW, a large convoy of the enemy was discovered coming close along the shore from the northward, under the protection of about twenty gunboats, and a numerous train of flying artillery on the beach. At three PM I made the signal to weigh and attack the convoy, and stood directly in for the body of them, then off the town of Rota; at four, the enemy's shot and shells from the gunboats and batteries going far over us, His Majesty's ships opened their fire, which was kept up with great vivacity until half-past six, when we had taken seven of the convoy, and drove a great many others on shore on the surf; compelled the gunboats to retreat, which they did very reluctantly, and not until two of them were destroyed; and actually silenced the batteries at Rota, which latter service was performed by the extraordinary gallantry and good conduct of Captain Searle, in the *Grasshopper*, who kept in upon the shoal to the southward of the town so near as to drive the enemy from the guns with grape from his thirty-two-pound carronades, and at the same time kept in check a division of gunboats that had come out from Cadiz to assist the others engaged by the *Alceste* and *Mercury*. It was a general cry in both ships, 'Only look how nobly the brig behaves!' The situation of our squadron was rather a critical one, tacking every fifteen minutes close to the edge of the shoal, with the wind in, and frequently engaged both sides. In the heat of the action, the First Lieutenant, Allen Stewart, volunteered to board the convoy, if I would give him the boats. I was so struck with the gallantry of the offer, that I could not refrain from granting them, although attended with great risk. He went, accompanied with Lieutenant Pipon and Lieutenant Hawky, of the Royal Marines, who most handsomely volunteered to go, as their party were chiefly employed working the ship; Mr Arscott and Mr Day, master's mates, Messrs Parker, Adair, Crooker, M'Caul and M'Lean, midshipmen; they were soon followed by the *Mercury*'s boats, under the command of the First Lieutenant W. O. Pell, accompanied by Lieutenant Gordon, and Lieutenant Whylock, Mr Ducain and Mr M. R. Cummings, master's mates. The boats, led by Lieutenant Stewart, pushed on in the most gallant manner, boarded and brought out seven Tartanes from under the very muzzles of the enemy's guns, and from under the protection of the barges and pinnaces of the Combined Fleet, which had, by that time, joined the gunboats. I was greatly indebted to Lieutenants Hickman and Jervoise (who both wished to go in the boats) for the spirited and well-directed fire they kept up from the main deck; also to Mr Westlake, the master, for his great attention to the steering and working the ship; and I have much pleasure in adding that the other officers, seamen and marines behaved with the utmost bravery and coolness. Captains Gordon and Searle (whose gallantry and excellent conduct it might be presumption in an officer of my standing in the service to comment upon) also report upon the great bravery and coolness of their respective officers, seamen and marines. It is with much pleasure I have to add, the frigates have received no material damage; the *Mercury*, an anchor shot away, her sails and rigging cut, though not much; our sails and rigging in the same way; but the *Grasshopper*, I am sorry to say, is a great deal damaged in the hull, the main topmast shot through, shrouds, sails and running rigging cut almost to pieces; she had one man mortally wounded, the gunner and two others wounded, but not severely.

'The captured vessels are all loaded on government account for the arsenal at Cadiz; and, I am happy to say, there is a very considerable quantity of valuable ship timber.

'The zest of this little service was greatly heightened by being performed in the mouth of Cadiz harbour, and in the teeth of eleven sail of the line.

> I have, &c.
> [Signed] MURRAY MAXWELL
> Rear Admiral Purvis, &c.'

Alceste's log provides some further information which supplements Maxwell's narrative, as well as a number of minor but interesting points on which it differs. It tells us, for instance, that Gordon's *Mercury* commenced firing at 3.20, followed by *Alceste* herself ten minutes later. The boats were sent in-shore at five, and at six the two frigates ceased firing so as not to interfere with their operations. By seven the boats were back with their prizes and an hour later the ships had returned to their anchorage. Later that evening Gordon and Searle came aboard for further orders, as did the temporary captains of the prizes. The mood of the conference must have been a combination of delight that the enemy had been so decisively foiled, elation at the prospect of prize money, and relief that what could have been a heavy butcher's bill was almost absurdly light.

Gordon's own log is brief and to the point, as befitting that of a subordinate commander, and merely confirms the facts of the engagement. Searle's cramped and untidy scrawl, however, reflects the pleasure he derived from his duel with the enemy's coastal artillery: 'Silenced the batteries twice and shott [*sic*] away their flagstaff and colours.' The Spanish horse artillery seems to have made little impression and it would not be unreasonable to assume that, having endured the concentrated weight of the warships' fire, seen guns and limbers smashed and their crews shot down around their weapons, that the blue-and-red coated gunners had limbered up smartly and galloped off to a more respectable range.

Maxwell's deliberate use of the word zest in his report gives some indication of the spirit in which the engagement was fought. It was indeed a very remarkable achievement on the part of some very remarkable junior officers, all of whom were extremely young. Thomas Searle, a future Rear-Admiral, was already known as something of a fire-eater, and only three weeks after grape from his guns had swept the interior of the battery at Rota, *Grasshopper* again emerged victorious from a desperate affray, winning for him his next promotion. A fine career also lay ahead of Gordon's First Lieutenant at Rota, Watkin Owen Pell, who would in due course be honoured with a knighthood and retire as an Admiral.

Maxwell clearly knew Gordon well from their time in the West Indies. They were good friends and rather similar in their outlook, preferring to lead by example while ensuring that their subordinates received every credit that was due to them; significantly, neither approved of flogging as a means of punishment, resorting to it in only the most extreme cases.

In the nature of things captains tended to be rather solitary individuals who could only relax in one another's company. Maxwell and Gordon dined together whenever possible but were often prevented from doing so by the weather. It has long been the custom in the Royal Navy to use the *King James Bible*, the *Book of Common Prayer* and *Hymns Ancient and Modern* for semi-official communications between ships, quoting chapter and verse as appropriate, but, as the following extract of signals between *Mercury* and *Alceste* shows, Gordon and Maxwell developed their own somewhat unusual means.

Mercury, 10 January:
'I'm sorely grieved and very low,
    Because it does so strongly blow,
To keep to windward isn't in her,
    Or in-shore I might have ate your dinner.'

Alceste, 10 January:
'Yes – I'm grieved to find,
    Ship holds so very bad a wind,
And get you – leave to go,
    Upon a lee shore. No, No, No!'

Off Rota, 4 April 1808

Mercury, 14 January
'The goose will still cut up for stew,
  Then come to dinner, oh pray do;
Decanted is Madeira wine,
  And there's no doubt the weather's fine.'

Maxwell had evidently initiated this exchange of dreadful doggerel, and in so doing caused muttering among Mercury's yeomen, for one of Gordon's early responses reads:

'When to make verse you do incline,
  Hoist a French Jack between each line!'

One further adventure in Cadiz Bay awaited Gordon. The brig *Ned-Elvin*, which had been captured from the Danes, came dangerously close to running aground among the breakers near the lighthouse. during the hours of darkness. Admiral Purvis sent his Flag Lieutenant and Spanish interpreter, Captain Hilton, with boats and tackle to retrieve the situation. 'Captain Gordon came on board as a volunteer,' recalled Hilton, 'to observe how affairs were conducted: and seeing that some broken water was in our track, he passed through it in his gig and signalled to me, as agreed, that there was sufficient depth. I thought it a bold measure on his part.' As a result of this, the brig was saved.

Gordon was rewarded for his share in the action off Rota when, on 22 August 1808 he left the elderly *Mercury* and assumed command of a comparatively new frigate, the *Active*, of 38 guns, with which he was to win even greater laurels in the Mediterranean..

NOTES

1. Forester would have been most unwilling to forgo such a splendid piece of theatre and returned to it on several occasions. The theme of immobilising a blockaded enemy squadron provided the major naval battle in *A Ship of the Line*. Hornblower, it will be recalled, had been rewarded for his services in the Pacific by being given command of a 74, the *Sutherland*, which, being Dutch-built, drew less water than her British counterparts and was therefore able to operate closer inshore. He took *Sutherland* into the fortified harbour of Rosas on the north-eastern coast of Spain with the intention of inflicting crippling damaged on a small French squadron blockaded there. He succeeded, but lost *Sutherland* in the process. One factor which ultimately convinced him that he must surrender the dismasted, sinking wreck which his command had become was the steady, sustained fire of two gunboats. Somewhat prior to the battle at Rosas, Hornblower had, by coincidence, spotted two enemy infantry divisions, accompanied by their artillery, marching along the coast road just north of Barcelona; *Sutherland* had closed in and the weight of her fire had scattered them with very serious casualties. But perhaps the greatest

coincidence of all was that the name of an elusive enemy privateer captured by *Sutherland* also happened to be that of Murray Maxwell's ship – *Alceste*.

2.   It is, perhaps, possible that the Rota gunboats may also have inspired an incident involving Midshipman Hornblower in 1796. On this occasion, however, for the sake of dramatic interest, the gunboats have become full-blown war galleys, which survived in some Mediterranean and Baltic navies well into the nineteenth century. The galleys could carry twice the armament of the gunboats and were bigger, faster and far more dangerous opponents when they were fighting on their own terms. Hornblower's first encounter with them took place, significantly, off Cadiz, but Forester moved the area of his main engagement with them into the Mediterranean, where they could operate at even greater advantage. During this action, Hornblower was quick to grasp the fact that the tactical answer to the becalmed *Indefatigable*'s problem lay in her own jolly-boat with which, by the greatest good fortune, he was able to capture one of the galleys.

On the other hand, as I have said earlier, Forester was not exclusively influenced by incidents in Gordon's career, and the naval history of the period is a treasure house of events in which truth often out-performs fiction. It seems more than probable that, as far as this episode was concerned, his thoughts were revolving around a remarkable incident in the career of the sloop *Speedy*, commanded by Commander Jahleel Brenton. On 6 November 1799 *Speedy*, armed with fourteen 4-pounder guns, was escorting two ships, a brig bound for Trieste, and *Unity*, laden with wine and spirits for the Mediterranean Fleet, through the Straits of Gibraltar. Suddenly, no fewer than twelve gunboats emerged from Algeciras, heading directly for the little convoy. Two of them were schooners armed with two 24-pounders apiece and the rest were feluccas carrying one 24-pounder each. So, as James Henderson points out in his book *Sloops and Brigs*, the weight of metal thrown by the Spaniards amounted to 336 pounds as against just 28 pounds from *Speedy*'s broadside. Nevertheless Brenton closed in on them, enabling the brig to break free and continue on her way. *Unity* sought to do likewise, but was quickly surrounded by the gunboats, which started to hammer her. Coming up from astern, *Speedy* ploughed through them with both broadsides blazing and every unemployed man firing muskets at the enemy oarsmen from point-blank range. With oars splintered or carried away and rowers sent sprawling, the Spaniards hastily abandoned their attack on *Unity*, which also made good her escape. The fight raged on for a further hour and a half, after which the gunboats ran for the shelter of their coastal defence batteries. *Speedy* lost only two men killed and one wounded, but was badly cut up in the rigging and had so many holes in her hull that she dare not risk heeling and was forced to run before the wind into Tetuan Bay where she repaired the worst of the damage. When she reached Gibraltar, Brenton asked the Governor, a General O'Hara, why the fortress's guns had not supported him when the action had taken place well within their range. O'Hara's astonishing reply was that he had arranged a sort of live-and-let-live with the Spanish Governor of Algeciras! In a more ruthless age, Brenton would have received the Victoria Cross and O'Hara a court martial.

Chapter 6
FRIGATE CAPTAIN: LISSA

Gordon took possession of the frigate *Active* (38 guns, 300 men) at Gibraltar on 27 June 1808 and was to command her for the next four years. She was undoubtedly his favourite ship and he seems to have been happiest while commanding her. He also seems to have enjoyed a special relationship with his officers and all his First Lieutenants left him as Commanders. By now a very experienced officer, he had the knack of spotting the good in most of the lower deck's hard cases and lead-swingers, getting the most out of them with good-humoured recognition and personal encouragement, but, as in any such group, there were undisciplined criminals whom he punished by flogging if there were no alternative.

Active was ordered to the Mediterranean and in this context a word of explanation is necessary. Napoleon, now at the peak of his abilities, had disposed of the Continental members of the Third Coalition in a brilliant series of campaigns, and with the Treaty of Tilsit (1807) had forced Russia into an unwilling alliance with France against the United Kingdom. The previous year he had also announced the introduction of his Continental System, prohibiting British trade with the mainland of Europe. The problem was that British goods were in demand. Smuggling was rife and when Portugal chose to ignore the system altogether the Emperor mounted an invasion in November 1807. This was followed in March 1808 by the forcible installation of his brother Joseph on the Spanish throne. In May, less than a month after the action off Rota, a national insurrection erupted across Spain, leaving French garrisons isolated. British aid, military and financial, was promptly dispatched to the Portuguese and Spaniards. The long Peninsular War, which Napoleon himself would regretfully refer to as 'The Spanish Ulcer', had begun.

In the Mediterranean, where the Royal Navy was firmly settled into its new base at Malta, there were several strands to British naval strategy. These included harassing the French along the coast of Spain, blockading Toulon, guarding Sicily, preventing a repetition of the French expedition to Egypt, and preserving access to the Adriatic. The last was a special case, for through Trieste and other ports smuggled British goods poured into central Europe. Through this channel also flowed financial assistance for Austria, a major participant in every coalition organised against Napoleon and whose armies, though defeated time and again, always came back for more. Again, in this area Napoleon was in direct contact with the Ottoman Empire, which he sought to overawe, and if he could be shown to be vulnerable, so much the better.

In theory the Adriatic should have been a French lake. The entire coastline of Italy to the west, the Gulf of Venice to the north, and the Illyrian and Dalmatian coastlines to the east were all firmly under French control. As for bases, Ancona, Venice, Trieste, Fiume (Rijeka), Ragusa (Dubrovnik) and Kotor were just some of the harbours available. The French Navy had a number of frigates based at Venice and Ancona, and also had at its disposal the small but efficient Venetian Navy. In addition there was a Russian squadron, consisting of four ships-of-the-line and two frigates, based at Trieste.

Unfortunately for the French, the roads in the area, particularly those along the eastern seaboard of the Adriatic, were so bad that most traffic, military and commercial, was carried in coastal vessels. Such a situation offered rich pickings for the Royal Navy, the more so when it was discovered that the commander of the Russian squadron was not really interested in implementing the provisions of the Treaty of Tilsit, and clearly the French and Venetians could not be everywhere at once. Furthermore, once the Ionian Islands, with the exception of Corfu, had been taken, they acted as a stopper to the Adriatic, in which the Royal Navy had established a central base on the island of Lissa, the present-day Vis. Light forces only were needed, usually frigates acting alone or in concert. These were the sort of conditions in which young, energetic captains, operating in virtual independence, could use their initiative, and the story of operations in the Adriatic is full of their captures, raids and cutting-out expeditions.[1] One such was Captain William Hoste, commander of the 32-gun, 18-pounder frigate *Amphion*, under whom Gordon would serve for much of the time. Hoste had been a protégé of Nelson's and he certainly possessed the Nelson touch. During his first cruise in the Adriatic, in company with *Unité* (Captain Patrick Campbell), he took no less than 218 vessels which provided the bulk of the £60,000 prize money he collected during the war. He and Gordon were about the same age and developed a friendship that contemporaries remarked was similar to that which had existed between Nelson and Collingwood. An inspired leader whose crews were devoted to him, Hoste was described by Lady Hamilton as 'a second Nelson', but whereas his manner could be uncomfortably direct, Gordon was said to possess 'the most equable temper, and his suavity of manner frequently carried him through difficulties with comparative ease, which the other would probably have found more labour in surmounting'.

On reaching the Adriatic Station Gordon discovered that while there were prizes aplenty to be picked up along the coast, many were too small to warrant sending back to Malta with prize crews and had to be burned or scuttled. Cumulatively, while the small prizes actually sent in contributed to his bank balance, he was involved in little of real note for some considerable time.

The morning of 28 June 1810, however, found *Active*, in company with Hoste's *Amphion* and a third frigate, the 32-gun *Cerberus*, commanded by Captain Henry Whitby, in the Gulf of Trieste, pursuing an enemy convoy laden with naval stores bound for Venice. When the convoy entered shoal water in which the frigates could not follow, Hoste sent his own boats in pursuit, at which the enemy sought refuge in the harbour of Groa. Hoste was not prepared to let the matter rest there. During the evening he signalled *Active* and *Cerberus* to

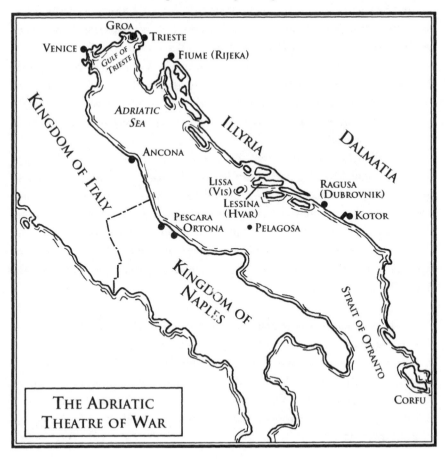

THE ADRIATIC
THEATRE OF WAR

concentrate their boats on *Amphion* at midnight for a major cutting-out expedition. *Active* was too far in the offing to be able to comply with the signal in time, but Gordon nevertheless decided to send in his boats as a second wave.

During the early hours of 29 June the main party's boats, commanded by *Amphion*'s Lieutenants William Slaughter and Donat Henchy O'Brien, and *Cerberus*' Lieutenant James Dickenson, pushed off and with muffled oars made for the shore.[2] A landing was successfully effected before first light a little to the right of the town, apparently without the enemy being alerted. But when the raiders crossed the headland separating them from Groa at dawn they were confronted by a company of the French 81st Regiment and a crowd of armed civilians occupying a favourable position. The confrontation was unexpected and when the French immediately opened a heavy fire, killing and wounding several men, Slaughter ordered the party back into the cover provided by some hillocks while he considered the next move. It was made for him by the enemy who, believing that the British were running for their boats, abandoned their position and came on with the bayonet, cheering wildly. They were received with steady volleys which dropped several of them before the fight became hand-to-hand. In the brief, savage mêlée that followed they quickly discovered that the Royal Marines were the handier with the bayonet and that a cutlass-wielding seaman with his dander up was not a man to be trifled with. Suddenly they broke and fled, leaving an officer, a sergeant and 38 privates as prisoners in the raiders' hands.

Slaughter advanced into the town and took possession of 25 vessels. While the original landing party were working aboard them, *Active*'s boats had beached and, led by Lieutenants Moore and Mears, their crews joined Slaughter. It was as well that they did so, for the surrounding countryside was in uproar and at 11 o'clock a 23-strong platoon of the French 5th Regiment, based at Maran, a village in the interior, entered the town to find out what was going on. Slaughter promptly led the *Active*'s men in a counter-attack and, to a man, the French flung down their arms.

'Every exertion was now made to get the convoy out of the river; but, it being almost low water, that object could not be effected before 7 p.m. and then not without great labour and fatigue, the men having to shift the cargoes of the large vessels into smaller ones, in order to float the former over the bar. By 8 p.m., however, the whole detachment and the prizes reached the squadron, which had anchored about four miles from the town.

'The loss on the part of the British, in performing this very gallant service, amounted to four marines killed, one lieutenant of marines, three seamen and four marines wounded, and the loss sustained by the French amounted to ten killed, eight by bayonet wounds, a proof of the nature of the conflict, and eight wounded. Of the captured vessels, eleven were burnt in the river, being too large to pass the bar in the state of the tide; five were brought out and sent to Lissa with cargoes, as were also 14 or 15 small trading craft, laden with the cargoes of the eleven burnt vessels.'

It was typical of Hoste that he should conclude his dispatch by commenting, 'No credit can attach itself to me, sir, for the success of this enterprise, but I hope I may be allowed to point out those to whose gallant exertions it is owing.' He then listed all the officers involved, giving their Christian as well as surnames.

This sort of depredation understandably generated immense pressure on the French naval commander in the Adriatic, Commodore Bernard Dubordieu, to do something about it. Dubordieu could count on no support whatever from the Russians, but he still had a considerable force at his disposal, including two French 40-gun frigates, *Favorite* and *Uranie*, the Venetian 40-gun frigate *Corona*, two 32-gun frigates, *Bellona* and *Carolina*, and two corvettes, *Jéna* and *Mercure*. But, rather than Dubordieu keeping an eye on Hoste, the reverse tended to apply and at length it was evidently suggested that the former might produce better results if he changed station. Accordingly on 29 September he left Chiozza with his squadron and arrived at Ancona a few days later.

Hoste, who had temporarily detached *Cerberus* to Malta, was watching closely from a point twelve miles north-north-west of Ancona with *Amphion* and *Active*. During the morning of 6 October the enemy squadron was observed to be making preparations for leaving harbour. By noon all the French and Venetian ships were out and clearly intent on pursuing the intruders, with one three-strong division on the starboard tack and the remainder close hauled on the larboard tack, ready to take advantage of any change of wind. Cheekily, Hoste steered straight for them, counting heads until he was convinced that the odds were too long, then tacked on to a north-easterly course at 1300 hours. Dubordieu continued the pursuit until 1400 hours, and then reversed course and returned to Ancona in rising seas and wind. Hoste followed and, having seen his opponents safely tucked up, set course for Lissa. Small wonder that the Royal Navy felt it could do as it liked in the Adriatic. Ironically Dubordieu was personally a courageous man and a keen student of his profession, which could not be said of everyone under his command.

Although Gordon was not a principal in these events, he was regularly in action and, as William O'Byrne comments in his *Naval Biographical Dictionary*, published in 1849, 'his prompt and zealous co-operation in the different services on which he was employed raised his name to a high pitch'. Indeed, throughout the year 1811 his name was to appear regularly in the *London Gazette*.

On 3 February 1811, while operating off the Italian coast again, this time under the command of Captain Whitby of *Cerberus*, four prizes were cut out of the harbour at Pestichi at the cost of one man wounded in *Active*'s boats. Nine days later Whitby and Gordon came across a convoy of ten merchantmen escorted by a small Venetian warship off Ortona. All eleven ships were captured and for good measure two large magazines on the shore were burned. It seems that the enemy contemplated a counter-attack on the landing party but were foiled when Gordon manoeuvred *Active* into a position from which she could give direct gunfire support, for Whitby comments in his dispatch, 'I feel particularly indebted to Captain Gordon for the judicious manner his ship was placed, by means of which he prevented any body of the enemy from forming in the rear of our men, and the promptness and zealous co-operation I have constantly experienced from him since we have been together.'

The Ortona raid was probably the last straw for the French. Dubordieu, having been reinforced, was ordered to eliminate the British presence at Lissa once and for all. On 11 March he sailed from Ancona with every warship at his disposal, plus an infantry battalion with which to occupy the island.

At about 0300 hours on 13 March *Active*, patrolling a mile or so off Port St George, spotted Dubordieu's ships lying to and, having made the night signal for 'enemy in sight', bore up to rejoin the squadron. By 0600 hours Hoste had formed line ahead with his own *Amphion* in the lead, followed by Gordon's *Active*, then the 22-gun *Volage* under Captain Phipps Hornby, and Whitby's *Cerberus* bringing up the rear.

For his part, Dubordieu was an admirer of Nelson's and, just as the latter had broken the line of the Franco–Spanish Combined Fleet at Trafalgar with two parallel columns, so now he intended to break Hoste's line with two columns of his own. The right column he led in his own flagship, *Favorite* (Captain La Meillerie), followed by *Flore* (Captain Villon), the Venetian *Bellona* (Captain Duodo) and a 16-gun brig, *Principessa Augusta*; the left column was led by Danaé (Captain Péridier), followed by two Venetians, *Corona* (Captain Pasqualigo) and *Carolina* (Captain Baratovich); in addition, but trailing behind the line, were one 10-gun schooner, one 6-gun xebec and two gunboats, all

Venetian. Single ship duels between frigates were commonplace, but a battle on the high seas between opposing frigate squadrons was almost unheard of, so what was taking place off the coast of Lissa that morning was something unique in naval history. The odds were very much in Dubordieu's favour: seven major units against Hoste's four; 284 guns against 156; 2,655 men against 879.

By 0900 hours, with the wind blowing from the north-north-west, the British line, battle ensigns streaming, was moving due west, back towards the coast of Lissa. Hoste ran up the signal 'REMEMBER NELSON', which was greeted with cheers from all his ships. By now the squadron had crossed the Franco–Venetian T and was engaging the leading enemy ships with full broadsides. In contrast, Dubordieu's columns, approaching obliquely from the northeast, had comparatively few guns that would bear. Furthermore Hoste, a canny fighter, had already guessed that Dubordieu intended to break his line.

Most captains had their idiosyncrasies, and Gordon was no exception. When in action, he preferred to command from well forward, laying his drawn sword on the capstan. Hoste, spotting him, hailed him over the stern: 'I say, Jemmy, pass the word to keep the flying jib-boom over the taffrail, for we must not let these rascals break the line; half an hour on this tack is worth two on the other!'

The significance of this became apparent very quickly. The British line closed up so that bowsprits came close to overhanging the stern of the vessel ahead as the line continued towards the coast of Lissa. Dubordieu's intention had been to force *Favorite* into the gap between *Amphion* and *Active*, but now, realising that he could not do so without placing his own ship in serious jeopardy, he decided to board *Amphion* instead and had his helm put

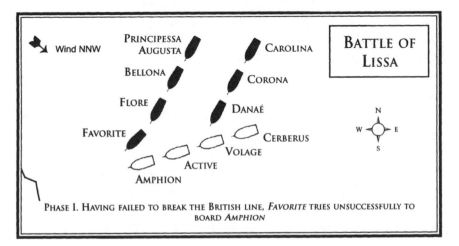

PHASE I. HAVING FAILED TO BREAK THE BRITISH LINE, *FAVORITE* TRIES UNSUCCESSFULLY TO BOARD *AMPHION*

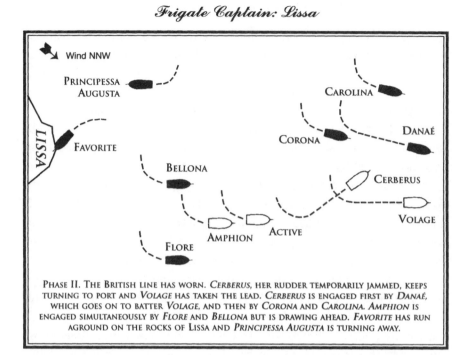

PHASE II. THE BRITISH LINE HAS WORN. *CERBERUS*, HER RUDDER TEMPORARILY JAMMED, KEEPS
TURNING TO PORT AND *VOLAGE* HAS TAKEN THE LEAD. *CERBERUS* IS ENGAGED FIRST BY *DANAÉ*,
WHICH GOES ON TO BATTER *VOLAGE*, AND THEN BY *CORONA* AND *CAROLINA*. *AMPHION* IS
ENGAGED SIMULTANEOUSLY BY *FLORE* AND *BELLONA* BUT IS DRAWING AHEAD. *FAVORITE* HAS RUN
AGROUND ON THE ROCKS OF LISSA AND *PRINCIPESSA AUGUSTA* IS TURNING AWAY.

over to starboard as the two ships closed. Large numbers of his crew could be
seen running forward in readiness but, once again, Hoste was fully prepared.
From somewhere he had procured a 5½-inch howitzer which he had mounted
on the forecastle.[3] Into this were crammed 750 musket balls so that when the
weapon was fired the packed ranks of the French boarders were sent sprawling
in bloodied heaps; among them lay Dubordieu, dead. Captain La Meillerie and
all the ship's officers were also down, save for a midshipman and the
commander of the troops, a Colonel Gifflenga. Neither was equal to the task.
For some minutes *Amphion* and *Favorite* were running parallel and then, at
0940 hours, with the shoreline only half a cable distant, Hoste hoisted the
signal for his ships to wear together. Seeing the danger, someone aboard
Favorite ordered the helm to be put up, but it was too late and the French
frigate piled herself on the rocks.

So far Hoste had every reason to be satisfied. He had disposed of one
opponent and his squadron, having reversed course, was now running east while
the enemy, having abandoned their attempt to break the line, seemed to be
conforming in a fragmented sort of way. But the critical phase of the battle was
only just beginning. *Flore*, next in line to the wrecked *Favorite*, crossed *Amphion*'s
stern and, seeing that he was about to be raked, Hoste ordered his crew to lie
down, and the broadside caused damage but few casualties. Hoste now found

himself engaged with two opponents, Flore and Bellona, positioned respectively on his starboard and port quarters. Elsewhere, *Cerberus'* rudder had been jammed by a shot when she wore and she continued to turn to port, and was out of the line, until the situation could be rectified. She was overtaken by *Volage*, which was now leading the much-extended British line. The enemy's left division now entered the action. *Danaé*, in the lead, shirked an encounter with *Active* by turning hard to port, and sought an easy victory over the much weaker *Volage* by running parallel and close aboard her, only to receive an unpleasant surprise when the latter's 32-pound carronades sent balls smashing through her side. Captain Péridier therefore opened the range beyond the reach of the carronades and proceeded to batter the smaller ship with his 18-pounder cannon. Aboard *Volage*, Captain Hornby responded by increasing the carronade charges, only to see them snap their breeching ropes or dismount themselves from their slides because of the heavier recoil. This left him a single long 6-pounder chaser on the forecastle with which to reply to the Frenchman and for a while *Volage*'s future looked very uncertain.

Cerberus, too, was in trouble. She had solved her rudder problem but was 90 men short of her full complement so that when *Corona* ranged alongside she was clearly having difficulty in matching her rate of fire. The third ship in the enemy's left division, *Carolina*, might have finished off *Cerberus* very quickly had she chosen to close, but she refrained from doing so, and merely contributed a few distant shots at the two leading British ships.

Throughout this phase *Active* was left without an opponent. Gordon, on the horns of a dilemma, needed to make a rapid decision. Should he return to assist Hoste who was beset by two enemy ships; or clap on all sail and go to the rescue of *Cerberus* and *Volage*? Astern he could see *Amphion* slowly drawing ahead of her opponents whose fire was consequently becoming less effective, and he decided on the latter course. This really altered the entire nature of the battle because when, at some time between 1000 and 1030 hours, *Corona*, *Carolina* and *Danaé* observed *Active* bearing down on them, they quickly disengaged and made off to the east under a press of canvas with Gordon in hot pursuit. *Cerberus* and *Volage*, their hulls shattered and the latter's rigging in tatters, could only heave to and repair the worst of their damage.

At about 1115 hours Hoste made the decisive move. He was some way ahead of *Flore* and suddenly came up into the wind so that his port broadside bore directly on the Frenchman's bow. After five minutes of heavy and sustained firing *Flore* struck her colours. Almost immediately *Bellona*, having passed her stricken consort, tried to rake *Amphion* through the stern. Some of

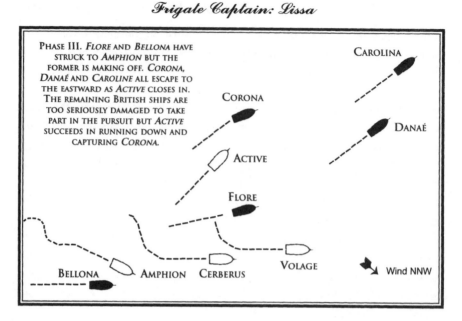

PHASE III. *FLORE* AND *BELLONA* HAVE STRUCK TO *AMPHION* BUT THE FORMER IS MAKING OFF. *CORONA*, *DANAÉ* AND *CAROLINE* ALL ESCAPE TO THE EASTWARD AS *ACTIVE* CLOSES IN. THE REMAINING BRITISH SHIPS ARE TOO SERIOUSLY DAMAGED TO TAKE PART IN THE PURSUIT BUT *ACTIVE* SUCCEEDS IN RUNNING DOWN AND CAPTURING *CORONA*.

CAROLINA

CORONA

DANAÉ

ACTIVE

FLORE

VOLAGE

Wind NNW

BELLONA   AMPHION   CERBERUS

her fire struck *Flore*, one of whose officers indignantly seized the French ensign, halyards and all, and, having waved it at *Amphion* to confirm that she had struck, pointedly flung it into the sea. *Amphion* had also come under fire from *Principessa Augusta*, but the latter hastily sheared off under the power of her sweeps once an 18-pounder had been brought to bear. Hoste was now free to concentrate on *Bellona*. He brought *Amphion* round on to the starboard tack and positioned her on the Venetian's weather bow, pouring in one or two broadsides until, at about noon, her captain also struck. Meanwhile, to Hoste's disgust, Flore could be seen making off to the east. Thanks to the damaged state of the rigging, it had not been possible for Amphion to launch a boat and take possession of her and whoever had succeeded the seriously wounded Captain Villon in command had taken full advantage of the fact. Hoste considered the act to be dishonourable, and indeed by the standards of the day it was surprising; on the other hand, at no time did *Flore* attempt to rejoin the fighting. Determined that *Bellona* should not similarly escape, Hoste had his repair punt hoisted out and sent it across with Lieutenant O'Brien and two seamen. Once aboard, O'Brien discovered that at the beginning of the action Captain Duodo had ordered two or three barrels of gunpowder to be placed in the bower-cable tier with a view to blowing the bottom out of the ship if she were forced to surrender. Duodo had been mortally wounded and his officers clearly did not approve of the idea, but for peace of mind O'Brien dispersed the powder train and left one of his men to guard the barrels.

Somewhat optimistically, Hoste had the 'General Chase' run up. Neither *Cerberus* nor *Volage* were in a condition to comply and, with all her lower masts shot through and her foremast close to tottering, *Amphion* herself would have been unwise to try. Nevertheless, miles away to the north-east Gordon's *Active* could be seen in pursuit of *Corona*, *Carolina* and *Danaé*, while astern, on the fading shoreline of Lissa, a column of smoke and flames marked the end of *Favorite*, abandoned and set ablaze by her crew; at 1600 hours the flames reached the magazine and the ship was blown apart by a tremendous explosion.

Gordon, meanwhile, had come up with *Corona* at about 1230 hours. For an hour and a quarter *Active* endured the fire of the Venetian's stern chasers without being able to make satisfactory reply, but at 1345 hours, off the coast of the enemy-held island of Lessina, she finally reached a position to leeward of her and a fierce duel ensued. Significantly, the issue could have been settled by the intervention of either *Carolina* or *Danaé*, but both were more interested in entering the anchorage, where they would enjoy the protection of the coastal defence batteries. After 45 minutes of hard pounding, Captain Pasqualigo, who had earned the sincere respect of the British, struck his colours.

On Lissa itself, the *Favorite*'s crew, still some 200 strong, had made for Port St George. Here lay two of *Active*'s prizes under the command of two of her midshipmen. Gordon had clearly put fire into the belly of his junior officers; rounding up their prize crews and some privateersmen, they summoned the straggling column of French seamen and soldiers to surrender, which, having had enough for one day, they did. Other matters immediately claimed the midshipmen's attention. Under cover of the battle that was raging at sea, the Venetian schooner had entered the harbour and a moored Sicilian privateer brig had actually struck to her. Rushing aboard the brig with some of their men, the midshipmen manned her guns and drove off the schooner before she could do any further damage to British and Allied shipping in the bay.

Hoste's victory was complete, but it had not been cheap. *Amphion*, as mentioned, had already sustained serious damage to her lower masts and, in addition, her larboard main yard-arm and mizzen topmast had been shot away and her rigging was severely cut up. Of her complement of 251, fifteen had been killed and 47 wounded, Hoste himself being wounded in the arm. The necessary repairs were heavier than could be undertaken locally, or even in the Malta dock-yard, and Hoste would shortly take her back to England for decommissioning.

Active had sustained comparatively little damage, her loss during the battle amounting to four killed and 24 wounded. *Cerberus* had had her mizzen topsail yard shot away and was badly battered in the hull. She also had the highest proportional casualties of any with thirteen killed and 41 wounded of the 160 men aboard. *Volage* was also badly knocked about, having had her main yard and fore topgallant mast shot away, her sails, rigging and masts cut up, and her port side completely riddled. Of a crew of 175 she had thirteen killed and 33 wounded, bringing total British losses in the action to 45 killed and 145 wounded.

Further lives would be lost in the immediate aftermath of the battle. At 2100 hours *Active*, accompanied by *Cerberus*, was towing the crippled *Corona* back towards Port St George when a fire broke out in the prize's main top. This quickly spread to the whole main mast and the surrounding rigging, causing such alarm that *Active* cut herself free. By 2330 hours the worst of the blaze seemed to have burned itself out and the remaining fires were brought under control by parties from *Active* and *Cerberus*, commanded respectively by Lieutenants George Haye and James Dickinson, who finally succeeded in getting the main mast over the side. Sadly this very dangerous work cost the lives of four seamen and a marine from *Active* drowned, and Lieutenant Haye severely burned, as were a midshipman and two seamen from *Cerberus*. *Corona*, now little more than a wreck, was safely brought in; she was eventually repaired and taken into service with the Royal Navy as *Daedalus*. *Bellona* was purchased as a troopship and re-named *Dover*.

Apart from the outright loss of three frigates, it is difficult to estimate the casualties of the Franco–Venetian fleet. Some 200 men from *Favorite*, we know, were captured, but that does not mean that the rest of those aboard her, about the same number, were all killed or wounded, for some almost certainly got away in the boats or were picked up by the smaller Venetian vessels. *Corona* sustained the loss of 200 killed and wounded; *Bellona*'s loss was 70 killed and about the same number wounded, and *Flore*'s would have been similar; *Danaé*'s would have been much lower, despite the fright she received from *Volage*'s carronades, and that of both *Carolina* and *Principessa Augusta* would have been negligible. Perhaps, therefore, the Franco–Venetian casualties amounted to as many as 500 killed and wounded and about the same number captured. This represented 38 per cent of those engaged, although many of those included would have been soldiers rather than seamen.

It must have been very difficult for the French to explain so complete a defeat by a force half their size. Colonel Gifflenga, who seems to have got away, did not even try, but instead composed a dispatch so divorced from reality that William James was provoked into passing the dry comment in his *Naval History*: 'If every officer commanding a detachment of troops on board a

French frigate could make up so good a story, it would be well for the glory of the French navy that he, and not the captain of the ship, should transmit the particulars of the action.'

According to Gifflenga: 'At daylight we perceived the English division, consisting of a cut-down ship-of-the-line and three frigates.[4] As a consequence chiefly of the lightness of the breeze, the ships went into action one by one. At 1030 hours, the masts of the *Favorite* having fallen, Enseigne Villeneuve informed me he could no longer steer the ship. We, at that moment, struck upon the rocks off the island of Lissa. I ordered the people to be debarked. I took possession of several vessels, and I caused the frigate to be blown up.

'The English, in their utmost distress, entered the port of St George, after they had set fire to the *Corona* and one of their frigates; the cut-down ship-of-the-line, after being wholly dismasted, ran upon the rocks of the island, and, in all probability, was lost. The result of this action is the loss, on our part, of two frigates, and, on the part of the English, of one frigate and one cut-down ship-of-the-line. It is the opinion of the sailors, that if Captain Dubordieu had kept his squadron together we should have got possession of two English vessels, although the enemy had two cut-down ships-of-the-line.' Further comment would not appear to be necessary.

Hoste could not have cared less what the French said to one another in private, but *Flore*'s escape still rankled. Two days after the battle he sent a letter by flag of truce into Lessina harbour demanding that the frigate be handed over. A curt reply was received to the effect that *Flore* had not struck her colours, which had been shot away, and that further correspondence on the subject should be addressed to the French government. Nevertheless the possibility of a cutting-out expedition clearly unsettled the French and a few days later they sailed for the safer harbour of Ragusa on the Dalmatian coast.

The news of Lissa was very well received at home. All four Captains received the Naval Gold Medal and their First Lieutenants were promoted to Commander.[5] Gordon was said by his daughters to have valued this award above all the other honours he received. In due course he received a letter from his father, now based in Gloucester.

'The feelings of a father, upon such a glorious achievement as the victory you have obtained over the enemy, with such fearful odds against you, can be better conceived than described, and I shall therefore not attempt it. ...The first information that an action had been fought in the Adriatic came through France, in which it was acknowledged they had lost two frigates. Well-knowing the intention of Captain Hoste and yourself to bring these gentlemen to action, I had no doubts as to the truth of it, although my mind continued in a most distressing state till we had Captain Hoste's letter some days before the dispatches arrived and banished all doubts as to your safety.'

Hoste also wrote shortly before *Amphion* was paid off at Deptford, commenting that he had declined a knighthood but been offered a ship whenever he wanted. In due course he would return to the Adriatic.

In the aftermath of the battle Gordon got along extremely with his prisoner, Captain Pasqualigo, nicknamed 'Come Along' by the British officers because these were the first English words he had learned and continued to use on every possible occasion. Gordon personally advanced him the sum of 2000 francs so that he could purchase various necessary personal items, subsequently recovering this through official channels. Pasqualigo was most grateful for the kindnesses he had received, and on his being exchanged some months later he sent Gordon, via the priest at Lissa, six gold epaulettes, two gold sword knots and ten yards of Venetian gold chain (lace), a most generous present.

NOTES

1. The Adriatic, with its different nationalities and conflicting interests, would have been ideal Hornblower territory. Unfortunately Forester had already sent his hero to the other side of the world in 1808 (*The Happy Return*) and the years 1810 and 1811 found him employed elsewhere (*A Ship of the Line* and *Flying Colours*). These three books, it will be recalled, were written shortly before the outbreak of the Second World War, and it was six years before Forester returned to complete the Hornblower cycle, using Gordon's life as his matrix. Hornblower, one feels, would have felt perfectly at home serving under Hoste in the Adriatic.

2. Donat Henchy O'Brien was a fire-eating Irishman who rose to the rank of Admiral. His book *My Adventures During the Late War* (1902), and *Escape from the French: Captain Hewison's Narrative 1803–1809*, edited by Antony Brett-James (1981) make interesting and exciting reading. A number of his adventures were also recounted by Anthony Price in his book *The Eyes of the Fleet*, see Bibliography.

3. The 5½-inch howitzer was a standard Royal Artillery weapon usually issued on the scale of one per field battery. In the normal course of events one would be unlikely to find such a piece of ordnance aboard a warship and where Hoste scrounged it from remains a mystery. Nevertheless, in this context it was clearly worth its weight in gold.

4. Cifflenga is referring to a class of ship known as *vaisseau rasé* in which one or more of the upper decks have been removed from a ship-of-the-line, usually to convert her to a frigate. All Hoste's ships were purpose-built frigates except *Volage* which was a frigate by courtesy only.

5. The Naval Gold Medal was instituted in 1795 for appropriate award to admirals and captains of ships. The admirals' medal was two inches in diameter and the captains' 1.3 inches. The obverse showed Britannia being decorated with a chaplet of laurel by Winged Victory, the reverse being engraved with details of the action and the recipient's name. After 1815 the medal was discontinued and successful senior officers received the Order of the Bath.

Chapter 7
FRIGATE CAPTAIN: PELAGOSA

For some weeks after the Battle of Lissa the Adriatic remained a British lake. Franco–Venetian morale had been so sorely affected that *Danaé*, *Flore* and *Carolina* put yet more distance between themselves and Lissa, retiring from Ragusa to Trieste. Perhaps this was as well, for with Hoste returned home in *Amphion*, and *Cerberus* and *Volage* both requiring prolonged repairs at Malta, Gordon's patched-up *Active* remained alone until replacements could be sent to join her. These included *Alceste* under Captain Murray Maxwell, whom we last met off Rota and who again became Gordon's superior, the frigate *Unité* (36) under Captain E. H. Chamberlayne, and *Acorn* (20) under Captain George M. Bligh.

During the period that the British squadron was being re-constituted, however, Gordon was far from idle. The last week of July found him operating off the Dalmatian coast, and on the 28th he pursued a convoy of 28 vessels laden with grain, bound for the garrison of Ragusa. This entire coastline is a maze of islands and channels in which to play hide-and-seek, and near the island of Ragosniza the convoy suddenly headed towards the mainland, hoping to conceal itself in a deep inlet. The move was detected and Gordon, dropping anchor, sent in his boats under Lieutenants James Henderson, George Haye (now recovered from the burns received aboard *Corona*), and Robert Gilson to cut them out. This they succeeded in doing at the cost of only four men wounded, burning ten of the vessels which were either not worth bothering with or for which there were insufficient prize crews available and returning with the rest.

Life for the British Squadron in the Adriatic continued much as before, and although little of note happened for several months Maxwell was aware that the French had assembled a strong force at Scisina which intelligence sources suggested would be used in another attack on Lissa.

During the night of 27/28 November heavy weather forced the British ships to seek shelter in Port St George. At first light the shutters of the telegraph station on Whitby Hill began blinking to the effect that three suspicious sails were in view to the south. This suggested two alternatives to Maxwell: either the French attack on Lissa was in the offing; or the Franco–Venetian squadron was making a run from Trieste to Corfu. Whatever was happening, he must ensure the security of his base while he investigated. A lieutenant, a midshipman and 30 seamen from *Alceste* and *Active* were detailed as crews for three prize gunboats lying in the harbour, and all three frigates contributed contingents of marines to man the two batteries which had been erected on Hoste Island, opposite the entrance to the port. Leaving overall command of the defence in the hands of Captain Bligh, Maxwell began the back-breaking process of warping *Alceste*, *Active* and *Unité* out of harbour in the teeth of a fresh east-north-east wind.

By 0700 hours the ships were at sea. At 0930 hours, off the south coast of the island, a strange sail was sighted to windward. The vessel fired two guns and hove to so that a boat from *Unité* could board her. She proved to be a neutral merchantman in which Lieutenant J. McDougall of *Unité* had taken passage to Malta the previous day. Several hours earlier the ship had spotted three French frigates some 40 miles to the south and McDougall had immediately obliged the master (by what means is not stated) to put about so that those on Lissa could receive adequate warning. With the prospect of action imminent, McDougall rejoined his own ship and the three British frigates set all the sail they could carry against the wind, which had now come round to east-south-east.

Nothing was seen of the enemy during the day, but at 0920 hours next morning *Active* signalled that she had three strange sails in sight to the east-north-east, off the island of Augusta. By 1000 hours it was possible to identify the strangers, who had formed line and were steering towards the British, as frigates. Those with an eye for detail were quick to observe that although they were not the Franco–Venetian squadron from Trieste, they had a French look about them, despite the lack of ensigns.

They were, in fact, the 40-gun frigates *Pauline* (Commodore Montfort) and *Pomone* (Captain Claude Rósamel) and the 26-gun frigate-built store ship *Persanne* (Captain Satie), on passage from Corfu to Trieste. That they had been at sea since the 16th, and the manner in which they bore down on Maxwell's ships suggests that they were anticipating a rendezvous with the Trieste squadron. In Adriatic terms a major naval operation was under way, and the reason for it was that *Persanne* had stowed aboard an extremely important cargo in the form of iron and brass gun barrels for naval and military use; rather more, in fact, than Napoleon was to deploy at Waterloo.

It did not take Commodore Montfort very long to discover his mistake. His ships suddenly altered course to the north-west and set their studding sails in an attempt to escape. Maxwell's squadron, cramming on an equal press of canvas, pursued. By 1100 hours it was apparent that the heavily laden *Persanne* could not keep up with her escorts and she made off to the north-east. Gordon made to follow, but the 'Recall' signal immediately shot up *Alceste*'s halyards; Maxwell would need *Active* when it came to dealing with the French frigates and he sent *Unité* after the transport.

At 1150 hours he signalled *Active* 'Remember the Battle of Lissa.' Neither Gordon nor his crew were likely to have forgotten, but it was well intentioned. At 1230 hours, with the rocky island of Pelagosa beginning to show some fifteen miles to the south-west, *Unité* and *Persanne* could be seen far to the east, exchanging fire with their bow and stern chasers.

By 1320 hours *Alceste* was closing on the enemy frigates in fine style and by Maxwell's reckoning she was bounding along at more than nine knots. His intention was to overhaul *Pomone*, leaving her for Gordon to deal with, and personally engage *Pauline*. The two ships had still not formally identified themselves, but Maxwell was sufficiently sure of their nationality to fire a single round into *Pomone*, sending splinters flying off her larboard quarter. The French ensign was promptly hoisted by both enemy frigates, *Pauline* additionally broke out a commodore's broad pendant.

What followed next came as a most unpleasant surprise. In general, French gunnery was not usually the equal of British, but some individual gun captains were obviously capable of producing remarkable results. *Pomone* replied with a single round, fired on the upward roll, and it splintered *Alceste*'s main topgallant mast. That might have been regarded as luck, but in view of what followed it evidently was not.

Still under full sail, *Alceste* began to overhaul *Pomone* at 1324 hours and both ships began exchanging broadsides. Maxwell was confident that he would come up with *Pauline*, the more so as the latter, seeing that she was outsailing her consort, had taken in her royals. At 1340 hours, while running directly abeam of *Pomone*, *Alceste*'s main topmast was shot through just above the cap. The wreckage, including the top-gallant and royal studding sails, came crashing down over the starboard side. While the tangle was being cut free the ship lost way, falling astern of Pomone. What galled Maxwell most was the barrage of derisive cheers and shouts of *'Vive l'Empereur!'* from both French ships. 'They thought the day their own,' he commented in his report, 'not aware of what a second I had in my gallant friend Gordon, who pushed *Active* up under every sail.'

Active came ploughing past and by 1400 hours, having reached a point on the starboard or lee quarter of *Pomone*, brought her to close action. Now the cumulative effects of experience and unending gun drill began to make themselves felt. Heaving, sweating, loading and ramming, the crews of Gordon's 18- and 9-pounder cannon and 32-pounder carronades slammed shot into the enemy hull at a rate the French could not match, although they fought back hard. This duel had been in progress for some 20 minutes when *Pauline* braced up, re-set her royals, wore round and stood for the weather beam of *Alceste*. By 1430 hours the two were also closely engaged.

Gordon was fighting *Active* from his usual position, standing on a shot rack beside the capstan. At about this time a 36-pound ball smashed through a gun port, grazed the carriage of a carronade, took off a seaman's leg and struck the Captain on the left knee joint, carrying it off as cleanly as if it had been done with a knife and leaving the lower leg hanging by tendons. Gordon recalled that he was not immediately aware of great pain, almost certainly because of the effects of shock, and he retained consciousness, so that as he was carried below he was able to tell Dashwood, his First Lieutenant, that he was now in command, and instruct Haye, the Second Lieutenant, who commanded on the main deck, to do his best should he have to take over in turn. Once below, Gordon declined attention until the seaman who had received similar injuries had been seen to. During the next few minutes Dashwood had his right arm shot off and Haye, though himself wounded, continued to fight the ship for the rest of the action.

At about 1450 hours a strange sail broke the horizon. It bore down towards the action and was identified as the British 18-gun sloop *Kingfisher*, drawn to the sound of the guns. The unwelcome appearance of the newcomer, and fact that *Pomone* was decidedly coming off worst in her duel with *Active*, convinced Commodore Montfort that he would do little good by remaining. By 1505 hours *Pauline* had all sail set and was standing away to the west. Shortly afterwards, *Active*, which still had all her topsails set, drew some way ahead of her by now waterlogged opponent and for a while all firing ceased. At 1540 hours, however, *Alceste* ranged alongside Pomone and opened fire with her starboard broadside. Almost immediately *Pomone*'s main and mizzen-masts went over the side and a British flag was hoisted to signify that she had struck. Captain Rósamel had undoubtedly fought his ship to the limit because shortly afterwards her shattered foremast also fell, and so riddled was her hull by *Active*'s shot that there was already five feet of water in the hold. She had sustained the loss of some 50 killed and wounded and there remained just sufficient time to take off her crew before she sank. Rósamel complained bitterly that Montford had left him in the lurch, but most of the damage had already been done before *Pauline* left the scene. He declined to surrender his sword to anyone but Maxwell, the senior British officer present. Maxwell was indeed entitled to the trophy, but as the lion's share of the work had fallen to *Active*, he took it across to her and presented it to Gordon.

During the engagement *Alceste* had one midshipman and six seamen killed, and one lieutenant, eleven seamen and one marine wounded; *Active*'s losses, in addition to those already mentioned, included one midshipman, five seamen and two marines killed, and twenty seamen three marines wounded. Neither ship was in a condition to pursue *Pauline*, which, it was subsequently learned, had reached Ancona in a very disabled state.

Meanwhile, *Unité* had also brought her part in the action to a satisfactory conclusion. For four hours *Persanne* had led her a merry dance, causing considerable damage to masts, spars, sails and rigging with her stern chasers, as well as seriously wounding one seaman. At length, at about 1600 hours, *Unité* had closed the gap sufficiently to open fire with part of her broadside. *Persanne* made a token reply in kind and then hauled down her colours, having sustained the loss of two killed and four wounded as well as a certain amount of damage aloft.

The overall consequences of the action off Pelagosa extended far beyond the immediate destruction of an enemy frigate and the capture of a transport. The loss of so many guns not only delayed the reconstruction of Franco–Venetian naval power in the Adriatic, but also meant that a number of French divisional commanders would have to scratch around to complete their artillery element. Of course it is impossible to estimate how many Allied lives might have been forfeit to those guns before the war finally ended, but the number might have been considerable and their capture provides an interesting reflection on the powerful indirect influence exercised by naval operations on the conduct of land warfare.

The damage sustained by *Active* at Lissa, though patched up, had been compounded to the extent that she would require preliminary repairs at Malta to restore her seaworthiness, and then a complete refit at home. Gordon would go with her and, as Maxwell's dispatch indicates, he would be sincerely missed: 'It is with poignant regret I inform you that Captain Gordon has lost a leg; but, thank God, he is doing well; his merits as an officer I need not dwell upon, they are known to his country; and he lives in the hearts of all who have the happiness to know him.'

Gordon received careful and expert attention from the ship's surgeon, Dr Stephen Jenner Swayne, with whom he developed a lifelong friendship. His own strong constitution bore him in good stead and helped him recover from the first effects of the amputation, enabling him to reflect philosophically that if he had to lose a leg, the left one was the one he could spare best because he had had several accidents with it and was already suffering as a result of stepping on broken glass, some of which had entered his foot. He certainly lost none of his sense of humour and would have been greatly amused by a lugubrious commentary in *Blackwood's Magazine*: 'A blasted French cannon ball carried off a leg hardly equalled in vigour by any leg in the service except by that one still remaining in his own possession!'

Much later in life, when he had attained high rank and stature within the Establishment, numerous stories were told regarding his achievements. One such, circulating in the smoking-room of the United Service Club, concerned the circumstances surrounding the loss of his leg and tells us something of the relationship which existed between him and his crew. On board *Active*, the story goes, was a pressed seaman who was trying to obtain his discharge on the grounds that he no longer had the use of one of his arms. When Gordon fell the man was among those who rushed to carry him to the cockpit, exclaiming, 'Oh, Captain, how sorry I am to see you have lost your leg!' To which Gordon was said to have replied, 'Thank you – how glad I am to perceive that you have found your lost arm!' In 1853 a Colonel Landwaun of Stoke Newington wrote to Gordon requesting verification of the story, which had been told to him by an Admiral Daly, and received the following reply:

'My Dear Colonel – I had forgotten all about the man in question until I saw in a newspaper some years ago a memorandum such as you have sent me; it was so nearly what took place that I did not think it worthwhile to correct it. I did press a man from an American ship who stated he could not use his arm but as, on examination, I found one arm as large as the other, I determined to keep him, telling him I could cure him. He was stationed and quartered on the quarterdeck to be under the eye of the officers – he was put in a boat and when that boat was sent away (on service) armed, he went in her, and his messmates were directed to watch him. I very often looked at his arm to see if it was wasted – if it had been I should have taken some other steps to oblige him to exercise it. After some months, I told him that when he thought proper to use his arm, I would give him the best vacant rating in the ship, ask no questions and never say a word of what had happened. You may remember that we were in action off Lissa on the 13th March 1811 and on the 29th November 1811, off Pelagosa, with the *Pomone*, where I lost my leg. I do not remember in which action this man used his arm, but I do remember seeing him working at his gun in action, going to him, putting my hand on his shoulder, wishing him joy, and sending for the clerk to order his being placed on the best vacant rating, and, until we were paid off, he was gunner's mate. I am quite certain he did not assist in taking me below, as I do not remember having such a conversation as stated by Admiral Daly, but at this time I cannot say whether I saw him using his arm in the first of the two actions or in the early part of the second.'[1]

There is no doubt that Gordon was a very popular figure and everyone was sorry to see him go, particularly in such circumstances. On 30 December, as *Active* was leaving the Adriatic on passage to Malta, she encountered *Eagle*, one of the ships-of-the-line maintaining a distant blockade in the Strait of Otranto, and Captain Rowley, her commander, used the occasion to pen a hasty note to him.

'My Dear Friend – I enter most warmly into your wishes not to be stopped in your passage and therefore will not detain you an instant longer than putting my letters of service on board of you; they are all ready, therefore the only detention is the moment of shortening sail. I congratulate you from my soul on your late gallant successes, and feel poignantly that your well and hard fought victories have placed the laurels on your brow with such severe loss; but, I trust in God you will soon recover, and for the sake of my country, I hope you will soon be enabled to aid her with your active service. Wishing you, my friend, a most speedy and quiet passage, I shall finish with assuring you of my high esteem, and of being your very sincere friend,

C. Rowley.

PS. I should have come on board, but I fear doing anything that may disturb and worry you. Not a line have I had these eight weeks from Malta. It is a pleasant state to be kept in!'

On arrival at Malta Gordon was to have been transferred to the Naval Hospital, but instead was accorded the generous hospitality of Colonel William Wood of the 14th (later West Yorkshire) Regiment, who saw to it that he received proper nursing in comfortable surroundings as his convalescence progressed. Worried that his family would be alarmed when the dispatches on the action off Pelagosa were published, Gordon had written to them as soon as possible. His father was particularly upset by the news, so he communicated further details through his sisters. In one letter he commented that his wound, left open to drain and heal from within after a stump had been formed, was now just two inches long and closing cleanly. Next, he learned to get about on crutches, but it was decided that he should wait until he had reached England before he was fitted with a standard wooden leg.[2] At the end of January 1812 he was heartened to receive a private letter from that former doyen of frigate commanders, Vice-Admiral Sir Edward Pellew, now Commander-in-Chief Mediterranean Fleet, written aboard his huge flagship, the 120-gun *Caledonia*.[3]

'Dear Sir – Altho' I received with infinite satisfaction and pleasure the reports of the very conspicuous and honourable share you and your brave shipmates bore in the recent gallant exploits in the Adriatic, which last year proved the field of still more successful efforts on your behalf; yet I confess I am unwilling, under the severe wound you are suffering, to make my letter the vehicle of congratulation, when regret for your misfortune and the loss the country will receive in your future exertions, call forth other sentiments from all those who feel for their country or who have the pleasure of being personally known to you. I have felt considerably relieved from my anxiety by the assurance of Sir P. Parker that you are in high spirits and doing as well as possible. I was still more pleased to hear from him you entertained no thoughts of leaving this country [i.e., the Royal Navy], which I most heartily hoped, as it will afford me great pleasure to avail myself of such conspicuous talents and bravery as you have exhibited on all occasions for the good of His Majesty's service.

I beg you to present my kind regards to your suffering Lieut. Dashwood, and believe me ever, with great esteem and regard, my dear Sir,

your faithful and sincere servant,

Ed. Pellew.

PS. My public letter will give you my intentions respecting *La Pomone*, and convey my public thanks to your gallant companions in arms.'

By degrees *Active* was restored to a seaworthy condition and in due course Gordon set sail with her for Chatham, where she was paid off in June. It was a sad parting for a Captain and crew who had been together for so long, shared so many dangers and achieved so much. As we shall see, neither was to forget the other.

NOTES

1. The opinion of Gordon's daughters was that the incident took place during the Battle of Lissa.
2. Known as a Greenwich Pensioner because of the number that could be seen in and around the Royal Naval Hospital.
3. Such importance was attached to the Mediterranean that in 1812 Pellew had under command no fewer than 29 ships-of-the-line, 29 frigates and 26 sloops.

Chapter 8
LYDIA AND *SEAHORSE*

W hen *Active* docked Gordon's brother Charles was there to meet him.[1]
The Gordon family, it will be recalled, while minor gentry, did not have
unlimited funds at their disposal and in 1801 he had entered the Royal
Artillery as a cadet, commission by purchase not being necessary in this branch
of the Army. He had undergone the rigorous training programme at the Royal
Military Academy, Woolwich, and received his commission two years later.
Promotion in the Royal Artillery was, in theory, by merit, but in practice seniority
ruled and progression was therefore slow. Nevertheless the Army's expansion
throughout the war had improved career prospects and Charles had recently
been promoted to 2nd Captain.

As far as the general public was concerned, the Royal Navy had always
been the more popular of the two armed services, although since its string of
victories in the Peninsular War the Army had begun to rise in popular esteem.
Charles himself was to embark for the Peninsula very shortly, and would see
active service at the defence of Cadiz, the siege of San Sebastián, the passage of
the Bidasoa, Nivelle, Nive and Orthez. For the moment, however, he had no tales
to tell and, when his brother was being fitted with his wooden leg, considerably
expressed himself envious, since it at least showed he had done his share.

In London the brothers were joined by their father, still in the
Paymaster's service but thinking of retiring on half pay to his holding in
Aberdeenshire, who had come up from Gloucester where he was based, and Mr
and Mrs Ward from Marlborough, bringing with them their daughter Lydia.

It will be recalled that a strong mutual attraction existed between
James Gordon and Lydia. It had been some years since they had met, and if they
corresponded during that period their letters have not survived. On the other
hand, she had sent him a lock of her hair by way of his sisters, with whom she
maintained a close friendship, and the fact that her parents had brought her to
London confirms that her feelings remained unchanged. No doubt there was a
degree of nervousness at their first meeting but it soon passed. Both had matured
and James was confronted with an attractive oval face topped with dark hair
worn up in the classical style with kiss-curls arranged symmetrically across the

forehead, fine eyes beneath well-defined brows, an extremely determined chin and a nose that a severe critic might describe as being just a shade too long, and possibly a little imperious.[2] A party was arranged to visit the theatre where the celebrated Mr Kemble was acting in *Coriolanus*, and during this James somewhat impetuously raised the subject of marriage. To his bewilderment and alarm Lydia made it clear that his attentions were not unwelcome, but said neither yea nor nay. Laying *Active* alongside an enemy warship must have seemed like child's play compared to understanding the ways of young ladies.

But the matter was not a simple one of womanly wiles. Marriages, even if not formally arranged, had to be seen as suitable, with each side contributing equally, both socially and financially. When the two had first met, James had been a young officer with limited means and an uncertain future while Lydia's family were firmly established; now, while Lydia's prospects remained unchanged, James had progressed far up the Captain's List, he had been decorated for gallantry, his future seemed assured and his finances were in much better order. Writing in 1890, his daughters commented that 'The proposal had to be made in a much more formal manner, and there is a very wide and striking difference from more modern customs in the deference with which Captain Gordon, accustomed as he was to perfect independence of action, and to rule and command, yielded to the advice and opinion of his relatives and friends. Besides the opinion of the parents on either side, Lord and Lady Glenbervie's sanction had to be obtained.' Today, such goings on might well turn the gentlest of girls into a raving virago, but Lydia accepted that these formalities had to be concluded and the custom must be judged of its time rather than our own.

The party broke up and returned to their respective homes with nothing apparently settled, leaving James thoroughly miserable. Fortunately, the details of what happened next are recorded in a letter from his sister Fanny to Lydia, written a few days later.

'My Dearest Lydia – Rawdon's letter to our dear James has made me love you, if possible, more than I have ever done, and I hasten to thank you for the happiness you have conferred upon him by permitting him to hope that the attachment which he has so long felt for you, is reciprocal.[3] You have relieved his mind from a world of care, my dear girl. You know "that he who greatly loves, must greatly fear", which is exactly dear James's case, and he could not be persuaded that it was possible you could think favourably of such a rough, uncouth mortal as he knows himself to be, and he returned from Town as miserable as possible, because he had not been able to open his heart to you as he wished, and he feared you were offended with him for saying what he did at the play. Charles and I both assured him that he had no great cause to be so miserable, as you could not have said more than you did in such a place, and if you had been very angry you would have told him! But I believe men in love have a pleasure in feeling miserable, for although he said yesterday that to be told you were disposed to listen to his addresses would make him the happiest of men, today, when he is assured of that, he says he cannot be happy without he has it from your-self, and he has made me promise to use my influence with you, my dear Lydia, to induce you to make him happy by writing, if only one line, to say you will accept his love and endeavour to love him in return. Do indulge him. He hopes to set off for Marlborough the beginning of the week, but as his going depends upon a man who is making a wooden leg for him, he cannot be certain. The one he got in Town has hurt him so much that he has been obliged to leave off wearing it: a very inge-nious man here [in Gloucester], who makes legs for the infirmary, has undertaken to make one which will be easier for him, but it cannot be ready before the end of the week, and perhaps not then, for the promises of trades people are seldom to be depended on. I have long known of James's attachment to you – indeed his only comfort was to write to me about you, praying me to tell you of his attachment, but I would not comply with his request, for I knew both our fathers wished nothing to be said on the subject till James should be in a position to enable him to marry, as they disapproved of long engagements. I want this house to be larger, that I may get you to come and see us, my dear girl. As soon as James can walk a little upon his wooden leg, I shall send him to sleep out of the house, and then we will take no denial. Believe me your ever, your truly attached friend, I hope soon to add Sister,

Frances M. Gordon'

Obtaining parental blessing was easy enough, but the Glenbervies were another matter. Gordon's career was now sufficiently far advanced that he no longer needed his uncle's patronage, but it would have been both ungrateful and discourteous not to have mentioned the subject. As Lord Glenbervie's letter indi-cates, he did not altogether approve of the match, but wisely chose not to oppose it, and indeed made arrangements for Gordon to receive an annual pension of £300 for the loss of his leg, so that the couple should have an additional income:

'My Dear James – I did not like to answer your letter until I had seen your Aunt. You well know that neither of us can have any wish concerning you but for your happiness, and to be united to a worthy, amiable and affectionate wife is the greatest blessing that can be enjoyed in this world. We have heard the most favourable report of Miss Ward, and your mutual knowledge of one another for so long a time is a very favourable circumstance. It would have been to be wished that the one or the other had been more gifted by fortune. But prudence and economy are, after all, the best fortune a woman can have. I sincerely hope the woman of your choice will be found to possess both. I should have agreed fully with your father in his advice that you should wait till you get a little richer, if I had not perceived that your own heart is so much interested on the other side of the question. As that is the case your present marriage will meet with the cordial approbation of your Aunt and myself. The only condition I should like to make with you and Miss Ward, if I felt myself entitled to make any, would be that you should not relax in your assiduous applications for immediate employment. I have received too advantageous an impression of her disinterested regard for your honour and interest to apprehend that she will suffer your union with her to interrupt your professional career, in which you have gained so much reputation and established so high a character, to say nothing of your duty to endeavour by pursuing that career to enable yourself to acquire such an addition to your worldly substance as may secure comfort and independence to you both, and to those who may come after you ...

Your most affectionate Uncle,

Glenbervie.'

Unwisely, James passed on the letter for Lydia and her parents to read. Her quite uncharacteristic response, written just four weeks before their wedding day, was glacially formal, partly because, protocol or not, she was seething with anger at Lord Glenbervie's comments; and partly because she had flatly rejected James's thoughtless suggestion that, after they were married, she should leave Marlborough and take up residence in his Aunt West's house, Sunny Bank, a mile from Aberdeen!

'I received your letter and its enclosure this morning, and can assure you my Father and Mother as well as myself, are much gratified by the kind manner in which your Uncle has written. It is now, I feel, too late for me to start any objection to your wishes for an early marriage. I must confess one principal obstacle is removed from my mind by my Father's having so kindly offered me to continue here as my home, during your absence. You may believe me he was much pleased to hear you had given up all thoughts of Sunny Bank, and I too am much obliged by your so readily acquiescing in my wishes on this subject. You did perfectly right in assuring Lord Glenbervie that it would not be my wish to prevent your fulfilling the duties of your profession, and however deeply I may, and most assuredly shall, feel our frequent separations, it would in my opinion be so entirely wrong, that I trust nothing will ever tempt me to influence you to give it up contrary to your better reason and judgement, but I shall look forward with hope to happier times, when you will be allowed to retire with honour to a situation of less peril.' James Alexander Gordon might be the most formidable antagonist imaginable at sea, but he had everything to learn about domesticity!

The couple's wedding at St Mary's Church, Marlborough, on the morning of 28 August 1812, was regarded as being sufficiently important to attract the attention of the *Naval Chronicle*. The bride wore a white silk dress brocaded with tiny pink rosebuds, which she changed for a dark-coloured habit when they posted to Bath that afternoon. After a few days together they returned to his father's house in Bell Street, Gloucester, where Gordon learned that he was required for sea service and would be taking command of the frigate *Pyramus* when she docked. For some unstated reason he did not welcome the appointment and went straight up to the Admiralty, where he succeeded in getting it changed to the *Seahorse*, then fitting out at Woolwich. At about this time Murray Maxwell returned home with *Alceste*. On 23 September Gordon wrote to Lydia, who was staying then with her parents in Marlborough.

'I have got a very snug little lodging, two rooms, and the old girl seems a good sort of fellow. I shall be with you on Sunday morning, but we shall be obliged to leave Marlborough on Tuesday, as the *Alceste* will then be paid off and I shall be the senior officer in the river, and must be there. I have been as much as possible with my friend Maxwell and his wife, and they are both very anxious to be acquainted with you, my dear girl. If you wish to be in London any time, you can stay there with Miss Rogers, and I can join you every night and come down in the morning.' Fanny wrote to Lydia the same day from Gloucester.

'I suppose you heard that the officers of the *Active* were to present James with a sword. It arrived on Sunday. I never saw anything so superb.

The handle is white ivory with embossed gold ornaments. The blade, a sabre shape, with the finest inlaid gilt devices on steel, such as Britannia, Fame and Hope leaning on her anchor, with all sorts of naval emblems, and on one side the following inscription – :This sword is presented to Captain J. A. Gordon, of HMS *Active*, by his officers, in admiration of his gallant conduct displayed on the 13th of March, off Lissa, and the 29th November, off Pelagosa." The scabbard in beautiful gilt – finished with a row of beads round the edge, which are large towards the bottom. The scabbard is open in several places, in which purple velvet is inserted, and upon which there are the most beautiful devices in embossed gold you ever saw. Hercules strangling the Nemean Lion, and in another part he is killing the Hydra-headed serpent with his club, and on one side is Neptune in his car, with his trident, etc., and to answer on the other side are James's arms, with the stern of the *Active* above, with flags and appropriate naval emblems, with cannons and carronades and chain-shot, and a thousand other things not to be described.'[4]

Meanwhile, the war continued. On 24 June 1812 Napoleon made the most disastrous mistake of his career by invading Russia, an error of judgement from which he never recovered. Five days earlier the United States had declared war on Great Britain. The publicly stated reasons for this included apparent British support for the hostile Indian tribes of the North-West Territories and the Royal Navy's continued impressment of seamen from American ships. Neither problem was insoluble given goodwill on both sides, but the country was expanding steadily and many leading politicians were determined to annex Canada while the United Kingdom was engaged in its apparently interminable war with France. The irony was that while America entered the war under the slogan 'Free Trade and Sailors' Rights', it would be American ship owners, seamen and merchants, hitherto the beneficiaries of the war in Europe, who would suffer most from it.

At this time the United States maintained a tiny regular army, about 7,000 men strong, and relied heavily on locally raised militia regiments. The latter would fight well enough behind defences but were unable to stand against regular troops in the field. Many of the senior officers to take the field were political appointees whose ambitions fell far short of the abilities. When the war began there were only 5,000 British regular troops in Canada, backed by Canadian fencible and militia units. The Canadians, it soon became apparent, had no intention of being annexed. In French-speaking Quebec Province, the language and customs of the people had been respected and no advantage was to be gained in joining a Greater United States; likewise the rest of the population contained a high proportion of loyalist families who, wishing to preserve their ties with the Mother Country, had moved north at the end of the American Revolutionary War and were violently opposed to the idea of being ruled from Washington. Thus, poorly led and indifferently motivated as they were, most American attempts to invade Canada ended in débâcle.

At sea, the story was very different. The United States Navy was small but professional, extremely efficient and had recently obtained valuable experience fighting against the Barbary pirates of North Africa. Knowing that they could not hope to match the Royal Navy on even terms, they had built no ships-of-the-line but instead planned for a *guerre de course* against British commerce, using frigates and smaller vessels. In this they were helped by having the services of one of the best warship builders of the era, Joshua Humphries of Pennsylvania, who set aside his Quaker beliefs to produce a unique class of heavy frigates, including the *Constitution*, *United States* and *President*. These could out-sail any likely opponent, and in favourable conditions could achieve up to 13 knots. Although nominally rated as 44-gunners, they could actually mount thirty 24-pounder cannon, twenty-two 32-pounder carronades, and chasers, giving them a far heavier weight of broadside than that fired by the average British frigate at long or short range. Furthermore, they possessed much thicker hulls that kept out most of the return fire. The seamanship, gunnery and discipline among the officers and crews of American warships was of a uniformly high professional standard. Indeed, one of the great paradoxes of this pointless war was that while British warships might number pressed American nationals among their crews, American warships certainly had British nationals aboard, including many who had deserted or sought to evade the press by enlisting in a foreign navy which offered better terms of service, and an even larger number of British-trained Americans who had been impressed into the Royal Navy at one time or another.[5]

The big American frigates quickly proved their worth in three single-ship actions. On 13 August *Constitution* sank the British frigate HMS *Guerrière* (38) in a 30-minute action off the coast of Nova Scotia. On 25 October, off Madeira, *United States* forced HMS *Macedonian* (38) to strike after she had been pounded into a near-wreck in a long-range gunnery duel lasting 90 minutes. On 29 December, off Bahia, Brazil, HMS *Java* (38) fought a skilful two-hour battle against *Constitution* before striking, having been so badly damaged that she was set on fire and allowed to sink. These losses caused consternation and a stiffening

Below: A somewhat idealised portrait of James Gordon at about the time he joined the Royal Navy, aged 11. Despite his angelic appearance, he was as much a handful as the Navy cared to cope with. (National Maritime Museum Negative D8458-A)

Centre: HMS *Arrogant* was Gordon's first ship. She is seen here a little later in her career, leading *Intrepid* and *Virginie* in pursuit of a Franco–Spanish squadron off the China coast, 27 January 1799. She has already clapped on all sail and her consorts are doing likewise. (National Maritime Museum Neg PAH9508)

Bottom: A crude water-colour representation of the final stages of Bridport's Action, 23 June 1795. Centre right is *Royal George* continuing the chase; centre left is the French *Tigre* which has borne up, having struck her colours, as has the *Alexander* on the extreme right. The last, formerly a British ship, was towed into Plymouth by the frigate *Révolutionnaire*, aboard which Gordon was serving. (National Maritime Museum Neg PU8507)

Above: The Battle of the Nile at the height of the action. Having led the British fleet round the head of the French line, *Goliath*, her ensign clearly visible, has dropped anchor beside *Conquérant*. To the right the French frigate *Sérieuse* is sinking; on the extreme left is the grounded *Culloden*. (National Maritime Museum Neg BHC0517)

Left: The portrait of the newly commissioned Lieutenant Gordon painted for his aunt, Lady Glenbervie, shortly before he joined *Bordelais*. He had already reached the towering height (for those times) of six feet three inches and was possessed of above-average fitness and strength. (National Maritime Museum Neg D8458-B)

Below: *Bordelais* tackling three French warships simultaneously, 29 January 1801. The brig *La Curieuse* is already sinking and boats are going to the assistance of her crew. On the left a second brig, *La Mutine*, and the schooner *L'Espérance* are making good their escape (National Maritime Museum Neg X1452)

Right: *Racoon* capturing *Lodi* off the coast of Haiti, 11 July 1803. A picture painted for Gordon's family to mark the event, which was a turning point in his career. (National Maritime Museum Neg D8458-C)

Centre: A cutting-out action – in this case the capture and removal of *Hermione* from the harbour of Porto Cavallo, 25 October 1799. Surprise was the key, but if it were not achieved the operation could become a desperate affair. Generally the attackers were divided into three parties: one to drive the crew below, one to cut the cable and one to make sail. Here boats are also being used to tow the ship clear of the harbour while, belatedly, the coastal batteries open fire on all concerned. (National Maritime Museum Neg A9970)

Bottom: The Battle of Lissa. Hoste closed up his line so tightly that the French could not break it. Having foiled an attempted boarding, he went about so suddenly that the French *Favorite* piled herself up on the island's rocks. During the final phase of the battle Gordon's *Active*, shown second-in-line, captured the Venetian frigate *Corona*. (National Maritime Museum Neg A7510)

Opposite page, top: Pelagosa. *Pomone* receives a pounding from *Active*. On the left *Pauline*, flying the enemy commodore's broad pennant, heads for safety while Murray Maxwell's *Alceste*, showing signs of some unexpectedly good French gunnery, steers to join in the duel. (National Maritime Museum Neg PU5812)

Opposite page, centre: Pelagosa. *Pomone* has been reduced to a sinking wreck. Aboard *Active*, Gordon has lost a leg, his First Lieutenant an arm and the ship is commanded by her wounded Second Lieutenant. Murray Maxwell insisted on presenting Gordon with the enemy captain's sword. (National Maritime Museum Neg PU5813)

Opposite page, bottom left: Captain James Gordon wearing his Gold Medal for Lissa. (Scottish National Portrait Gallery)

Opposite page, bottom right: Lydia Ward at the time of her marriage to Gordon. The portrait bears a striking resemblance to that of the fictional Lady Barbara Wellesley, itself based on Forester's description, contained in C. Northcote Parkinson's *Life and Times of Horatio Hornblower*. (National Maritime Museum Neg D8794)

Above: Early American successes during the War of 1812 caused serious alarm in the Royal Navy. They stemmed partly from professionalism and partly from a class of superbly designed frigates, one of which, the USS *President*, is seen here at the time of her capture in 1815. (National Maritime Museum Neg 663)

Above: A London cartoon published shortly after the brief British occupation of Washington. President Madison (fourth left) takes flight, pursued by the angry comments of his countrymen. The two seamen and the warship represent Gordon's expedition up the Potomac. (Anne S. K. Brown Military Collection, Brown University Library)

Left:. One of Gordon's principal opponents during the Potomac operations was Commodore David Porter, USN. (Courtesy US Army Garrison, Fort Belvoir)

Below: 24-pound cannon ball, 194-pound mortar shell and shell fragment, all fired by Gordon's squadron and subsequently recovered from the shoreline at Fort Belvoir, 1959–61. (Courtesy US Army Garrison, Fort Belvoir)

Above: A sketch from the Porter family history showing the American defences at White House, later the site of Fort Belvoir. (Courtesy US Army Garrison, Fort Belvoir)

Below: The unsuccessful bombardment of Fort McHenry, Baltimore, above which the huge American flag can be seen flying. To the fort's left is Baltimore harbour and, immediately to its right, the distant North Point. Close to the fort is one of the sunken blockships that formed part of the harbour defences. The scene was painted by an eyewitness to the event, Alfred J. Miller, who has captured the great range at which the engagement was fought, together with the unusual rig of the bomb vessels, to the right of which is the rocket ship *Erebus*. (Collection of the Maryland Historical Society)

Above: Chatham Dockyard at about the time Gordon was Superintendent. A number of hulks are visible, as well as vessels fitting out, and, in the foreground, a small steam paddle tug. After his wife died, Gordon would take his children for walks along the long anchor wharf, centre left, where one of *Active*'s old anchors was stored. (National Maritime Museum Neg PU1036)

Below left: The Royal Naval Hospital, Greenwich, where Gordon spent the last 28 years of his life, first as Lieutenant-Governor, then as Governor. (National Maritime Museum Neg BHC1822)

Below right: Portrait of Rear-Admiral Sir James Alexander Gordon, KCB, by Andrew Morton (1802–45), shortly after his appointment as Lieutenant-Governor at Greenwich. In due course he would rise to the rank of Admiral of the Fleet; the GCB would be added to his decorations; and when the Naval General Service Medal 1793–1840 was distributed in 1849, his mounted the greatest number of engagement bars ever issued. At the time of his death he had served in the Royal Navy for more than 75 years.

of resolve within the Royal Navy, unequalled for another century when, following the loss of a second battlecruiser during the early phases of the Battle of Jutland, Vice-Admiral Sir David Beatty commented, 'There seems to be something wrong with our bloody ships today – engage the enemy more closely!'

In 1812, as after Jutland, identifying the problem produced its solution. There was nothing wrong with the British frigates or their crews; they had simply been outgunned by bigger, better-protected frigates carrying much larger crews. In Second World War terms, each of the three encounters has been compared to a contest between a cruiser and a pocket battleship, although perhaps a 6-inch and an 8-inch cruiser respectively would be a closer analogy. The answer was to start building even larger frigates than the Americans, plans for which had existed since 1810. The new frigates entered service in 1814 and in the meantime three ships-of-the-line were razed as a stop-gap, retaining their sail plans for the sake of speed.[6] In the event, confidence was restored when, on 1 June 1813, the evenly matched HMS *Shannon* and the USS *Chesapeake*, both 38s, fought a duel off Boston, ending with the latter, one of the US Navy's class of smaller frigates, striking after fifteen minutes.

So it was in this climate of uncertainty that Gordon made *Seahorse* ready for sea.[7] In November 1812 she was detailed as part of a strong escort for a large convoy bound for the West Indies. She remained off Falmouth, waiting for this to assemble, and was then prevented by adverse winds from sailing until well into December. This enabled Lydia to visit the ship on several occasions, being hoisted aboard from a boat by means of a boatswain's chair. For the first time since he joined the Navy some twenty years earlier, Gordon was unhappy about going to sea. Obviously, he missed his new wife and, equally, he resented the pain and restriction caused by his artificial leg. Likewise, his new crew did not yet measure up to that of *Active*, and he was inclined to find fault with his superiors.

He and Lydia wrote regularly to each other during this period. They were affectionate letters revealing how deeply each cared for the other. She tells him to 'stay out of the rigging' and, having spoken to someone about the less healthy aspects of life in the West Indies, warns him 'I should not be very happy if you were as fond of wine as you are of SNUFF, and as to fruit, you should be sparing.' For his part, he promises her that 'nothing but necessity will ever oblige me to go above the deck', assures her that he is familiar with the dangers of the West Indies 'and will avoid everything that can hurt me in such a climate' and promises 'to leave off snuff'.[8] 'I have taken to Mr Drake's leg,' he says a few weeks later. 'And it answers so well that I think, after a little pain, I shall feel as comfortable in it, as I did in the other.'

He is also greatly concerned for her financial security. 'My agent has directions to remit to you my pension as soon after it is due as possible, but I must tell you it is only paid half-yearly, and the first half-year is due the 25th of December. I have also sent him an order to pay your drafts on them, but just now he has not a balance in my favour. However, I have written to him to inform you when you may draw upon him, and recommend you to do so, as what money you do not want to use may be laid out to the best advantage by buying into the Stocks in my name at Coutts. I have not yet been able to make up the money required by my marriage settlement, but I have directed Mr Abbott, of Clement's Inn, to pay my proportion of the *Pomone* into Coutts.'[9] And again: 'I have written to Fanny to beg her to tell my Father to pay you the rents on my large property in Scotland. I believe it is about £45 a year.'

Lydia, nevertheless, remained quite capable of putting her foot down when the occasion demanded it, and did so strongly regarding a house he proposed renting at Nettlestone on the Isle of Wight, conveniently situated for Spithead. Startled by the scale of her defiance, he wrote: 'Though you do not stomach my styling myself your lord and master, you know I am, and must tremble in my presence!' Sadly, her reaction to that is not recorded, but the upshot was that a house at Nettlestone was rented, though possibly not the one he had intended.

In the meantime, he is busy knocking his crew into shape, writing on 28 November: 'This afternoon we have been trying how our lads handle the guns, and I am happy to say they do better than I expected, though I do not think we are equal to a good action yet.' Ten days later there had been a marked improvement and he was able to comment: 'We have made the ship something like a man-of-war since we have been here [Falmouth] and if we do not sail for a week to come I think we will give a very good account of any enemy we meet.' Desertion remained a problem: 'I am sorry to say three of our men attempted to swim to shore last night. We just got hold of one of them as he was sinking. The others, of course, went down.'

By 18 December the convoy was under way, its route taking it south to Madeira and then across the Atlantic to Barbados. During the first week, trouble developed aboard one of the transports. 'We have had an opportunity of assisting an officer's wife with a little fresh provisions, as the ship she is in, with her husband and two small children, sailed in so great a hurry that they had no time to get any sea stock on board, and to make it more uncomfortable for the poor creature, the men that are on board are lads sent out to the condemned regiments, who have already put one officer to death, and fired at another.[10] I have desired them [the transport's officers]to keep close to us, and if those lads do not behave, I must try what the cat will do.'

At Barbados, the convoy split into smaller groups and *Seahorse* escorted her portion to Jamaica. 'We are all sorry to see that the Americans have taken another of our frigates. I wish one of our frigates which has been several years in commission would fall in with one of theirs. Eight years, my much beloved wife, make a great change in such a country as this. Many are dead, and several of the merchants whom I have seen living like kings, are not worth a copper now, from the effects of the war. A few years' peace may set them on their legs again. Several of my people have run away. I hope I may not get hold of them, as I must try them by court-martial. The Admiral, Stirling, is much disliked by every person, and has done several things which have induced people to talk in a strange way about him.'

Regarding the last, Gordon wrote again in February 1813. 'Admiral Stirling is a man I never did like, and never can. He came on board yesterday to look at my ship's company, as I had told him I thought them weak. He talked to them a great deal, and I believed frightened them so much, that they, to the number of fourteen, were determined to be off from the ship, but fortunately, after firing a few shot at them (they had got off in the barge), they came back, and all but six got in without our being able to learn who they were. Of course, my duty obliged me to flog them.'

It was, perhaps, in keeping with Stirling's somewhat unusual style of command that, returning to Port Royal in mid-March following a cruise, Gordon should learn from the Jamaica papers that *Seahorse* would be returning to England with a shipment of merchants' money. He wrote to Lydia telling her that this would earn him a handsome commission, but commented that as the packet was due to sail only a day ahead of *Seahorse* he expected to arrive before his letter. On 5 May he was in the Channel and sent a note ashore.

'My Dearest Lydia – I have only time to say I am off this port – Plymouth – on my way to Portsmouth, six weeks from Jamaica, with merchants' money, which will give me nearly £4,000. I am now so happy in the prospect of seeing my much beloved wife so soon that I can hardly write. As soon after you receive this as you can, put yourself, and anyone you can get to come with you, into a post-chaise and go to Portsmouth, where you will find me at the Crown. As the wind is dead against us, I do not expect to get there for three days, which will give you a little time. I will take lodgings, as my ship wants some repair, that would prevent it being

pleasant on board for some time. I have written to Fanny, and I hope she
and my father will come and see me.'

The reason Gordon insists that his wife be accompanied and that she travel by
post-chaise rather than stage-coach is that she is expecting their first child. To his
regret he was soon back at sea, on blockade duty off Cherbourg. He wrote indignantly that his Commodore, Milne, not only had his wife and two children
aboard *Venerable* with him, but also a maidservant. 'What do you think of that?
How officers can act so contrary to their orders I know not.' He also reports on
the progress of Lydia's youngest brother, Charles, whom he has taken to sea, and
on 9 July commented approvingly that he had just given a Mr Gordon 'a good
thrashing. I am sorry to say that Mr Gordon is a very bad boy, and few of the
lads speak to him.'

On 25 August Lydia sent a short note to him, ending: 'Thank God
with me for all His mercies, my dearest husband, here I am safe in bed with a
dear little girl by my side.' The christening took place almost immediately. 'On
Friday our little girl went to church, when she received the names of Hannah
Frances. My father, mother and Fanny are the sponsors. I cannot say much for
the prettiness of either of the names, and Hannah is, I think, one of the ugliest in
the whole list of Christian names, but I daresay we shall like it better now.'

Some weeks passed before Gordon learned that he was a father,
because *Seahorse*, in company with *Royal Oak*, had been sent on a sweep around
the British Isles in a fruitless search for small American warships and privateers
that were preying on commerce in home waters. The sweep, which extended as
far north as the Faroe Islands and as far west as St Kilda, included the Shetland
Islands and the west coast of Ireland, where several men from both ships
deserted. Then, with the autumn gales blowing hard, it was back to the endless
routine of blockade duty off Cherbourg, punctuated by periodic returns to Spithead, with *Seahorse* running short-handed because of desertion and sickness. By
11 November, as his letter to Lydia indicates, Gordon's morale had sunk to the
lowest point it was to reach in his entire career. 'I am in a very bad humour
today; the boatswain is sick from drinking too much, the carpenter is a fool, the
gunner I think I shall quarrel with before night; in short, I have given them all a
rub. I must tell you what I am afraid you will hardly believe – I would give up
my ship in ten days if I thought we had enough to live on ashore. We have been
in a heavy gale, and close to the French coast. If it blows in the morning, I intend
to run to the Downs, as my rigging gets very slack. The Commodore must have
been mad when he sent me to sea. Just now I feel much hurt by the conduct of

the Admiralty; I have only two years more, certainly not more than three, and I do not think the Admiralty will be very ready to give me a ship-of-the-line if they have an excuse for paying off this ship.[11] Oh! it is a bad one – these long, dark nights. I dine at half past two, go to quarters at four o'clock, and as it is dark a little before five, I have too long an evening without my dear little wife.'

Within three days the black mood had passed. For the first time since he had taken command Seahorse had fired her guns in anger and the result, as he describes, was the destruction of the 16-gun French privateer *La Subtile*. 'On Friday night we stood over for the coast of England. We made sail about half past six. A lugger was close by us, but as she had no sail set we took her for a Flushing boat. As day broke she was observed to go on the other tack and begin to make sail. Of course, we immediately wore and made all sail. We began to fire, and the foolish fellow persisted for three hours in trying to escape. At last, two shots struck her below water, but before we could get [out] our boats she went down and we were only able to save 28 men out of 65. We must have killed a great many. We buried four of the men who died yesterday after they were brought on board, and we have another who is desperately wounded – Swayne says he cannot live above five days. I shall anchor off St Helens to set my rigging up and send the prisoners to the flagship.[12] My friend Dashwood thought the Admiral was displeased with him for taking a privateer – what will he be with me?[13] The Admirals do not share for the head [prize] money of vessels taken, so he will make nothing by me. Charles sends his love. He will give an account of our capture; he never saw so many poor fellows sent to their last homes in so short a time before. I like my new marine officer very much. I think him a good soldier and he will make something of our troops. I am glad to say my people have not given much trouble, and there is only one poor fellow on the black list, which is an uncommon thing.'

And so the blockade continued throughout the winter. 'I do not like this cold, wet weather, and the stove smokes so much at sea that I am obliged to have it put out.' The misery between decks can only be imagined. On 20 November close observation of Cherbourg revealed that the French had launched two ships-of-the-line and two frigates, and that a sloop and a brig had left the harbour since *Seahorse*'s last visit. The new ships, Gordon recorded, 'Appear to be quite ready for sea, but from the way they get their topmasts up I do not think they have many men.'

This was a telling observation. The French Navy had been stripped of manpower to make good some of the losses incurred by the Army during the disastrous campaign in Russia. Time was running out for Napoleon. The Peninsular War was lost and now most of Continental Europe, including Austria, Prussia, Russia and Sweden, was arrayed against him. Throughout the year and on into the early months of 1814 he displayed flashes of his earlier brilliance but there was no turning the tide. On 31 March Paris fell to the Allies and eleven days later, at the urging of his Marshals, Napoleon abdicated unconditionally and was transported aboard a British warship to exile on the island of Elba. On 24 April the King of France, Louis XVIII, embarked aboard the yacht *Royal Sovereign* at Dover and, waved off by the Prince Regent, sailed to take possession of his kingdom.

The long war with France, it seemed, was over, though that with the United States would continue. So although the blockading squadrons at last returned to their home ports and the first steps towards demobilisation were taken, there was still plenty of work for the Royal Navy to do.

NOTES

1. His brother Sylvester had died in Ceylon in 1803.
2. This description could well be of Lady Barbara Wellesley, the Duke of Wellington's fictional sister, who first encountered Horatio Hornblower in *The Happy Return* and became his second wife. Forester would have found Lydia's portrait and letters among Gordon's papers, and, together, these seem to have suggested the sort of heroine he was looking for. It was, therefore, quite natural that he should have paid her the private tribute of naming Hornblower's ship *Lydia*.
3. Rawdon was Lydia's elder brother.
4. Actually, his father's arms, the following description of which was taken from one of his book plates, date about 1798: motto above crest 'In hoc spes mea'. Quarterly: 1st and 4th azure, a lion rampant argent between three boars' heads erased or; 2nd and 3rd azure three boars' heads erased or within a bordure engrailed argent. Shield with crest (a crosslet fitchée gules): no helmet; floral and other ornamentation – all against an oval shaded background.
5. According to Roosevelt's *Naval War of 1812*, between five and ten per cent of American crews were of British origin. The same source indicates that well over 6,000 Americans had been impressed by the Royal Navy; on the outbreak of war 2,548 of them refused to serve against their country and were imprisoned. It is not stated how many British seamen aboard American warships refused to serve.
6. One such was *Goliath* in which Gordon had served at the Nile.
7. *Seahorse* had a distinguished history. On 27 May 1802 she had taken the French frigate *La Sensible* (36) off Malta. On 5 July 1807, Great Britain and the Ottoman Empire having come to blows when the latter, under immense diplomatic pressure from the French, closed the Dardanelles to Russian shipping, she fought an epic battle against the Turkish warships *Badere-I-Zeffee* (52) and *Aliz Fezzan* (26). Heavily out-gunned and out-manned, she sank *Aliz Fezzan* and, after a protracted engagement reminiscent in several respects of *Lydia*'s duel with *Natividad*, forced *Badere-I-Zeffee* to strike. She had, however, been paid off in June 1811 and as the United Kingdom's manpower resources were seriously stretched, her new crew clearly left much to be desired.
8. His success was only temporary and he was to amass a large collection of snuff boxes during his lifetime, mainly gifts from friends.
9. Pellew had evidently decided on the award of prize money. See previous chapter.

10. Any regiment sent to serve in the West Indies regarded itself as being 'condemned' because of the high mortality rate. At this period the Army was sending the best of its reinforcements to Wellington in Spain; those sent to the West Indies were often of lesser quality and could contain a criminal element. Such men believed they had nothing to lose and obviously had to be watched very closely until they settled down.

11. Logically the next step in his career would have been command of a ship-of-the-line. Evidently the matter had already been discussed and the outcome was not to Gordon's liking. Furthermore, he was on poor terms with his Commodore and is only too aware of the deficiencies in *Seahorse* and her crew. Worst of all, he was worried that unless he obtained a more important command during the next two or three years his seniority on the *Captain's List* would mean virtual retirement on half pay.

12. St Helens was an advanced anchorage for Spithead off the east coast of the Isle of Wight, to which *Seahorse* returned after her spells off Cherbourg. It was within sight of the rented house at Nettlestone and Gordon tells Lydia that the ship's tender flies a small blue/yellow/blue pendant, 'so that if you see one with such a thing, you will know she has either been or is going on board the *Seahorse*'.

13. Dashwood, it will be recalled, had been Gordon's First Lieutenant in *Active*, and now had his own command.

Chapter 9

THE COMMODORE

For the United States, the downfall of Napoleon was an unmitigated disaster since it meant that the entire British war effort would now be directed across the Atlantic. In July 1814 the hard-fought battles of Chippewa and Lundy's Lane showed that, properly trained, American regulars could stand up to their British counterparts in the field, but their results were inconclusive and the prospect of annexing Canada was even more remote than it had been before the war began. Worse, thousands of Wellington's battle-hardened Peninsula veterans had already embarked and would soon make their presence felt in Canada and elsewhere.

At sea the situation was no better. The Royal Navy's blockade of the eastern seaboard was almost total, bringing international commerce to a complete standstill. Equally serious was the dislocation of local shipping, for in a country of vast distances and an as yet incomplete road system, the distribution of raw materials and manufactured goods relied heavily on coastal and river craft. The alternative, transport by land, was both painfully slow and prohibitively expensive, even where it was possible. The result was a general shortage of goods accompanied by an inevitable increase in prices, which affected everyone. So unpopular had this pointless war become that in the mercantile states of New England there was serious talk of leaving the Union.

Nor was the American Navy able to influence the situation. On dark, stormy nights the occasional warship or privateer might slip out of harbour and evade the prowling blockade squadrons to prey upon British commerce, but that was of little direct help to those at home. Again, as most American seamen preferred the greater rewards to had by privateering, the Navy was suffering from a manpower crisis so serious that some of its ships, including the *United States* and her prize the *Macedonian*, were decommissioned and lay abandoned in backwaters for the rest of the war.

British strategy in 1814 was centred on the building up of overwhelming strength in Canada prior to launching an invasion of the United States from the north, while simultaneously mounting a series of amphibious operations along the eastern seaboard that would divert American strength into the threatened areas. Of these, Chesapeake Bay was by far the most important. Indeed, the experiences of the Revolutionary War, the War of 1812 and the American Civil War all confirm that the side which controlled the Bay and its rivers at critical phases had an enormous strategic advantage and was the more likely to win.

British warships under the command of Rear-Admiral Sir George Cockburn had dominated Chesapeake Bay for much of 1813. Cockburn was described by Forester as being harsh and overbearing, to which he might have added completely insensitive. He ranged the length and breadth of the Bay, taking four privateers, capturing numerous small craft, and destroying anything and everything that might be of the slightest use to the American war effort. Although he could only afford to detach a maximum of 400 seamen and marines for landing parties, these met little or no opposition from the local militia, who generally fled before any serious fighting could take place. Cockburn, however, needed to obtain constant supplies of fresh water and beef to feed his men. In Spain Wellington had paid promptly and in gold for anything he needed, and a visit from his purchasing agents was always welcome. Cockburn, on the other hand, could only offer Treasury bills, redeemable in London after the war, which were of no use at all to Virginia and Maryland farmers with more immediate financial problems. Whether the latter accepted Treasury bills or not, their herds were driven off willy-nilly. This caused such outrage that landing parties were regularly sniped at by civilians willing to risk the dire penalties for engaging in hostilities, contrary to the established customs of war. In strict legal terms, such men placed themselves beyond the protection accorded to uniformed troops and could be hanged if captured. Cockburn was not the man to take a wider view and, if he could not lay hands on the snipers, he burned their farms and villages. This made him few friends, but the Americans still welcomed the numerous deserters from the British ships who swam ashore in the hope of making a better life for themselves in the New World.

British attitudes to the Americans varied in proportion to their distance from the fighting, as is frequently the case in war. At home there was a substantial body of opinion which regarded them as renegades who had chosen to stab their Mother Country in the back by siding with Napoleon. Those actually fighting the war, on the other hand, while disapproving of Washington's political ambitions regarding Canada, had a great deal of sympathy for those Americans caught up in the war. One such was Lieutenant-Colonel Charles James Napier of the 102nd Regiment, who expressed himself forcefully on the subject:[1] 'It is quite shocking to see men who speak our language brought in wounded; one feels as if they were English peasants and that we are killing our own people. Strong is my dislike to what is perhaps a necessary part of our job, namely plundering and ruining the peasantry. We drive off all their cattle – it is hateful to see the poor Yankees robbed.' Others, in both the Navy and the Army, had American relatives and their attitude was understandably ambivalent.

Nevertheless American behaviour in Canada had been less than impeccable. York (now Toronto), the capital of Upper Canada, had been burned to the ground, leaving hundreds of people homeless in the depths of the Canadian winter, and a number of smaller communities, including Newark (now Niagara-on-the-Lake), had been similarly razed. Such were the depredations on the Niagara front that many Canadians, like their American counterparts around Chesapeake Bay, had taken to guerrilla warfare in the form of sniping. The Canadians had also demanded official retribution, and in planning his strategy for 1814 Admiral Sir Alexander Cochrane, Commander-in-Chief of the North American Station, took full account of this, issuing the following order to his squadron commanders:

'You are hereby required and directed to destroy and lay waste such towns and districts upon the coast as you may find assailable. You will hold strictly in view the conduct of the American army towards His Majesty's unoffending Canadian subjects, and you will spare merely the lives of the unarmed inhabitants of the United States. For only by carrying this retributory justice into the country of our enemy can we hope to make him sensible of the impropriety as well as the inhumanity of the system he has adopted.'

With the arrival of the Peninsular War veterans Cochrane was also aware that it would be possible to strike at much larger objectives.

One weapon which would be extensively used during the forthcoming campaign was the rocket, developed by Colonel William Congreve at the Royal Arsenal, Woolwich, in 1804. There were various types of rocket, including incendiary, common shell, case shot and even parachute release, and they came in all sizes from little 6-pounders through 42-pounders to 13-inch monsters. They were incredibly cheap to produce (a 32-pounder and a 13-inch incendiary cost respectively £1. 1s. 11d. (1.10p) and £1. 17s. 11d. (1.80p) each), were easily transportable, could be fired from a light iron trough or even an earth bank, and had a maximum range of between 2,200 and 3,200 yards, depending upon launch elevation and size. Their major disadvantage was unpredictability because in flight they were neither stabilised by fins nor spun by angled exhaust vanes, a curious omission for so enthusiastic and thorough a man as Congreve. They were, however, ideally suited for employment against area targets and had been successfully used by the Navy in 1806 to bombard Boulogne, with such devastating results that not a shot was fired in return, in 1807 against Copenhagen, when they had caused a major conflagration, and in 1813 by Cockburn against Havre de Grâce. The Army had also shown an interest. A British Rocket Troop had been attached to the Swedish Army at the Battle of Leipzig and they were also used at Lundy's Lane. Many field commanders, Wellington included, disliked rockets because of their inaccuracy, but against inexperienced troops this in itself could be an asset. To some extent the course of cannon balls could be predicted, but that of rockets could not; they changed direction without warning, trailed flame and smoke, made a fearful noise and blew up with a thunderclap, showering shards of metal or case shot on those in their vicinity. Nor was the ancient axiom that the safest place to be was the target area applicable, for occasionally one would fly straight and true to achieve the desired result.

Once the blockade of the French coast had been withdrawn, Gordon's *Seahorse* underwent a brief refit and made up her crew. Gordon seems to have had the pick of the newcomers, for from this point onwards there was a different atmosphere aboard the frigate and he became very much his old self. Warned for service in American waters, he took a painful farewell of Lydia and his daughter, not knowing when he would return.

August 1814 found *Seahorse* in Chesapeake Bay where Cockburn's local knowledge was being put to use in planning a large-scale raid against Washington. The main thrust would involve a landing force under Major-General Robert Ross being put ashore from the River Patuxent and marching overland on the American capital. The secondary effort, which would also serve as a diversion, would entail a squadron under Gordon's command sailing up the Potomac to Fort Washington, a few miles downstream from Washington, and bombarding it. This undoubtedly gave Gordon much greater satisfaction than command of a ship-of-the-line because it not only restored the potential for independent action which he enjoyed so much, but also made due recognition of his seniority with the appointment of Commodore.[2] A second diversion was to made near Baltimore by Captain Sir Peter Parker in *Menelaus*.[3]

The significance of Gordon's role will be the better understood if that to be played by Ross is described first. Ross, whom Cockburn would accompany, had been among the best of Wellington's brigade commanders in the Peninsula, and his preparations were extremely thorough. He had at his disposal four regular regiments: the 4th (later The King's Own (Royal Lancaster) Regiment);

21st (later the Royal Scots Fusiliers); 44th (later The Essex Regiment); 85th (later The King's Shropshire Light Infantry) – which, having beaten the French in Spain and southern France, had rather hoped they might be going home and were now more than a little disgruntled at finding themselves off the American coast. These, together with artillerymen, marines and seamen, gave him a little over 4,000 men. Horses did not travel well by sea and, possessing neither artillery teams nor cavalry, he made alternative arrangements. It was correctly anticipated that, once ashore, comparatively few horses would be picked up, but those that were would be given to the artillerymen who, being horsemen already, would act as the landing force's cavalry. For artillery he decided to rely on rockets, one of which could be carried by each infantryman if no transport could be commandeered for the heavy boxes, and two 3-pounder pop-guns, which could be man-hauled.

Cockburn's ships and the transports carrying Ross' landing force entered the Patuxent on 18 August. Some opposition was encountered from a flotilla of gunboats and armed barges commanded by Commodore Joshua Barney, but the Americans were heavily outnumbered and withdrew upstream to Pig Point. Here Barney blew up or burned his craft and set off with his seamen for Washington. The officer responsible for the defence of the American capital was Major General William H. Winder, who had already been involved in one shameful débâcle in Canada which should have resulted in his being cashiered.[4] Instead, his political influence was such that he had not only survived but been promoted into the bargain. Aware that Ross' troops had landed at Benedict on 19 August, he marched his militia regiments to an intermediate position covering Fort Washington.

Ross was in a hurry, but the long weeks at sea had taken the edge off his troops' fitness and, in broiling heat, the first day's march left numerous stragglers along the way. On campaign, even the normal marching pace was much faster than it is today, and when, to accelerate progress, the famous Moore Quickstep was invoked, cross-straps constricted the chest, denying the lungs much-needed air, causing rapid exhaustion.[5] Nevertheless the pace was not relaxed and on 21 August the column reached Nottingham. On the 22nd Ross feinted in the direction of Fort Washington, causing such alarm that Winder hastily decamped and withdrew towards the capital. Ross, however, changed direction and by evening was in Upper Marlborough. The next day's march, a comparatively short one, brought him to Old Fields and here many of the stragglers caught up. By now the regiments were swinging along as they had in Spain so that on the 24th the advance on Bladensburg, where the East Branch river

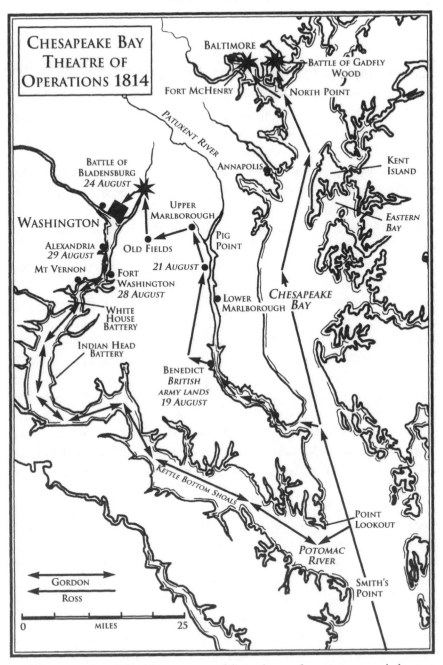

CHESAPEAKE BAY THEATRE OF OPERATIONS 1814

BALTIMORE

BATTLE OF GADFLY WOOD

FORT MCHENRY

NORTH POINT

PATUXENT RIVER

ANNAPORIS

KENT ISLAND

BATTLE OF BLADENSBURG *24 AUGUST*

UPPER MARLBOROUGH

EASTERN BAY

WASHINGTON

PIG POINT

ALEXANDRIA *29 AUGUST*

OLD FIELDS

MT VERNON

21 AUGUST

FORT WASHINGTON *28 AUGUST*

LOWER MARLBOROUGH

CHESAPEAKE BAY

WHITE HOUSE BATTERY

INDIAN HEAD BATTERY

BENEDICT *BRITISH ARMY LANDS 19 AUGUST*

KETTLE BOTTOM SHOALS

POINT LOOKOUT

POTOMAC RIVER

SMITH'S POINT

GORDON

ROSS

0   MILES   25

could be crossed and Washington entered from the north-east, was carried out at a cracking pace. At Bladensburg, Ross' advance guard, some 1,500 strong, found Winder's army, numbering about 6,500 militia and some guns, drawn up beyond the river, and went into action at once. An early attempt to rush the bridge resulted in casualties from the American artillery, but the stream was found to be fordable and the British had soon established themselves on the far bank. This unsettled the untrained militia, among whom Winder's orders and counter-orders had inevitably begun to produce disorder. The arrival of the rockets settled the issue very quickly. The first few flew high, but the remainder, laid on the ground, went shrieking past the militiamen's heads. This was too much for them and they broke *en masse*, leaving Commodore Barney's seamen, 370 in number, 78 marines under Captain Miller and a handful of regular soldiers, to make a very gallant stand until they were overwhelmed. During the Battle of Bladensburg the Americans lost 26 killed, 51 wounded, about 100 taken prisoner, and some 20 guns. British casualties amounted to 64 killed and 185 wounded, mostly at the hands of Barney's little detachment.

That evening the British troops entered Washington and the following day, as a reprisal for the destruction of York, they burned the uncompleted Capitol, the 'President's Palace' on Pennsylvania Avenue, and every public building except the post office.[6] Captain Thomas Tingey of the US Navy had already set fire to the Navy Yard and to two recently completed warships, the 44-gun frigate *Columbia* and the sloop *Argus*, to prevent their falling into British hands. Cochrane's order 'to destroy and lay waste' was pointedly ignored by Ross and his officers and even Cockburn was at pains to assure private citizens that their property would be respected. And so it was, the only house to be burned being one at the north-west corner of Maryland Avenue and Second Street North-East, from which a volley of shots left one British soldier dead, three more wounded and killed Ross' horse beneath him; when the house was cleared those responsible had fled.

Some of Washington's citizens had been half expecting an orgy of rapine and looting, but nothing of the kind happened and, furthermore, they were left in possession of their homes. So when the invaders began marching out that evening, they willingly assented to Ross' request that they should look after those of his wounded who were too ill to be moved. The landing force marched back to Benedict the way it had come and on 30 August was once more aboard its ships. But within 48 hours of Ross' departure from the capital, the shouted news in its streets was that the British were coming back, this time up the Potomac. Gordon's squadron, too, had reached its objective.

In addition to his own *Seahorse*, the ships under Gordon's command included the frigate *Euryalus* (36), commanded by Captain Charles Napier, otherwise known as Black Charlie, who was his Second-in-Command;[7] the bomb vessels *Devastation*, *Aetna* and *Meteor*, commanded respectively by Captains Alexander, Kenah and Roberts; the rocket ship *Erebus*, Captain Bartholomew; and the *Anna Maria*, tender and dispatch boat.[8]

Between Washington and the sea wound the wide Potomac, with several shoal areas along its course. It presented no serious navigational difficulties, provided that one knew the channels, and quite large merchantmen regularly used the port of Alexandria, although, significantly, when one of the large American frigates made the passage, she did so very slowly and with her guns lifted out. Gordon's principal difficulty at this phase of the operation was that the only available charts were unreliable and, of course, a pilot was out of the question.

The squadron got under way from its anchorage in the river mouth on 17 August. It kept to the Virginia shore and by the following evening had reached the Kettle Bottom shoals where *Euryalus* stuck fast. Napier took soundings fore, aft and all round which, to his astonishment, showed deep water everywhere. He sent over a diver who reported that the ship was resting on an oyster bed the size of a boat. Once this had been cleared the frigate was hauled off. Gordon was not so fortunate. *Seahorse* ran so hard aground that ten of her guns had to be lifted out, together with a large quantity of stores, before she could be pulled free. This, together with the work of reloading, took the better part of a day. Several of the smaller ships also grounded but were freed without too much difficulty.[9]

The squadron had barely cleared Kettle Bottom when the wind veered to a contrary direction and remained there. Five days of back-breaking warping and towing followed, during which the ships covered a mere forty miles. During this time, curiously, not one shot had been fired at them from the tree-lined shores. The evening of the 25th found the squadron anchored off Maryland Point. As darkness closed in the sky to the north was illumined by a huge, flickering glow which marked the destruction of Washington's public buildings and Navy Yard. Ross had evidently succeeded in his mission and Gordon now had to decide whether his own was still relevant; as a diversion would still be useful while Ross marched back to his ships, he decided that it was.

Next day, while the ships were warping into the Maryland Reach, they were struck by a sudden and violent squall. *Seahorse* had her mizzen-mast sprung but *Euryalus* was more seriously damaged, her bowsprit and the head of her foremast being badly sprung and the heads of all three topmasts carried away. Gordon seriously considered aborting the mission until Black Charlie assured him that *Euryalus* would be fully rigged by the time the rest of the squadron arrived. His marines manned the boats and took her in tow while the seamen were setting up new rigging. Darkness brought the work to a temporary standstill, but by 1300 hours on the 27th, just as the squadron's two sternmost vessels passed, *Euryalus* was ready for action again.

At last the wind became favourable which enabled the ships to continue upstream under easy sail. On the Virginia shore the elegant mansion of Mount Vernon, once the home of George Washington, came into view, as, some distance beyond on the opposite bank, did Gordon's objective, Fort Washington. Originally known as Fort Warburton, it had been re-named and strengthened in July 1813 and now had twenty 18- and 32-pounder guns in the main works, and eight 32-pounders in a water battery. In command was an artillery officer, Captain Samuel T. Dyson.

Gordon intended to soften up the defences that evening with a bombardment by his bomb vessels. Under cover of this, *Seahorse*'s Master, Lothian, was sent to sound the channel with an escort of boats. If Lothian's report were favourable, the frigates were to engage the fort at close range next morning and a strong party would be landed to storm the defences, covered by more bombs and a rain of rockets from *Erebus*.

Not a shot greeted the approach of the British ships, although figures could be seen scurrying about in the fort's embrasures. The three bomb vessels moved into position, dropped anchor and sprung their cables. There were only a dozen or so such vessels in the Navy and they were the only warships to carry explosive shells aboard, with elaborate but very necessary safety precautions. They carried a few small guns but their main armament consisted of one or two heavy mortars in fixed mountings that were reinforced below to absorb the recoil. Direction was obtained by use of the anchor springs and range by adjusting the size of the charge in the mortar; the point in the trajectory at which the shell exploded was determined by the fuse setting, the fuse itself being lit by the ignited propellant; all of which required considerable experience, skill and judgement of such other factors as wind. Because the use of bomb vessels was so highly specialised, their officers at least tended to be enthusiasts.

Several shells were thrown into the fort without any response. There was then a sudden and much heavier explosion within, suggesting that one of them had penetrated the magazine. It had not; the magazine had been blown up by Dyson himself, who was drunk, and the activity in the embrasures had simply been his men spiking their guns before making good their escape. At first light on the 28th the landing party took possession of the fort, the interior buildings of which had been demolished by the explosion, and thoroughly wrecked the gun-carriages and anything else that might be of use.

Gordon was of the opinion that the fort could 'have done us much damage',", and indeed even with the inadequate garrison at his disposal – some eighty men – Dyson could have made life very unpleasant for a while. Asked to explain his actions, he said that the verbal orders he had received from Winder, through a Major Hite, on the 24th, were that: 'in case I was oppressed by, or heard of, an enemy in my rear, to spike our guns and make my escape over the river. The enemy approached by water on the 27th, and we learnt that day, through several channels, that the enemy had been reinforced at Benedict, 2,000 strong, and that they were on their march to co-operate with the fleet, in addition to the force which left the city. Under all the circumstances, the officers under my command were consulted and agreed that it was best to abandon the fort and effect a retreat. The force under my command was thought not equal to a defence of the place.'

Much of this was the product of fevered imaginations. Again, however one construed the term 'rear', the nearest British troops were many miles away, intent only on regaining their ships. At his court-martial Dyson was found guilty of several appropriate charges and dismissed the service; he was also found guilty of conduct unbecoming an officer, though strangely not that of a gentleman.

With the destruction of Fort Washington, Gordon had more than fulfilled his mission, but he decided that the situation could be exploited by the capture of Alexandria, six miles further upstream. By 1000 hours *Seahorse* was within sight of the port, in which several merchant vessels were already lying on the river bed, their owners having opened their seacocks in an attempt to prevent capture. Soon a boat was seen approaching under a flag of truce, carrying a deputation from the town council.

Alexandria was a prosperous mercantile port that had once rivalled New York and Boston. Prior to, and indeed since, the Revolution, George Washington and other leading figures of Virginia and Maryland society had ordered fashionable clothes, textiles and household furnishings of every kind from England through its merchants, and the comparatively recent decision to site the new capital of the United States nearby had added to its prosperity. The present war, however, had caused serious damage to its trade and, moreover, the townspeople were aware that they were vulnerable to attack. On their behalf representatives of the council had repeatedly spoken to Winder, and once to President Madison, with a view to having defensive works constructed downstream. Much had been promised but nothing had been done save the strengthening of Fort Washington. The town itself was more than prepared to do its patriotic duty. It had raised its quota of militia, both infantry and artillerymen, but they were now in the field; it had spent $1,500 on mounting its own cannon, for which no ammunition had been provided. Earlier that very month three of its banks had lent the government $50,000 for the purpose of erecting proper defences; the money had been paid, but, as usual, nothing had been done. Now Fort Washington had fallen without firing a shot and Alexandria lay at the British squadron's mercy.

The worried deputation came aboard *Seahorse* and asked Gordon what his intentions were. He told them he would communicate his terms in due course, but in the meantime assured them that in the absence of hostile acts from the townspeople, they and their property would not be harmed. During the day the rest of the squadron came up and dropped anchor along the entire length of the waterfront. Next morning, the 29th, Gordon set out his terms:

'Gentlemen – In consequence of a deputation yesterday received from the city of Alexandria, requesting favourable terms for the safety of their city, the under mentioned are the only conditions in my power to offer:

'The town of Alexandria (with the exception of public works) shall not be destroyed, unless hostilities are commenced on the part of the Americans; nor shall the inhabitants be molested in any manner whatever, or their dwelling houses entered, if the following articles are complied with:

1.   All naval and ordnance stores (public and private) must immediately be delivered up.
2.   Possession will be immediately taken of all the shipping, and their furniture must be sent on board by the owners without delay.
3.   The vessels that have been sunk must be delivered up in the state they were in on the 19th August, the day of the squadron passing the Kettle Bottoms.
4.   Merchandise of every description must instantly be delivered up; and to prevent any irregularities that might be committed in its embarkation, the merchants have it in their option to load the vessels generally employed for that purpose, when they will be towed off by us.
5.   All merchandise that had been removed from Alexandria since the 19th instant is to be included in the above articles.
6.   Refreshments of every description to be supplied the ships and paid for at the market price by bills on the British government.

7.   Officers will be appointed to see that the articles Nos 2, 3, 4 and 5 are strictly complied with, and any deviation or non-compliance on the part of the inhabitants of Alexandria will render this treaty null and void.

'I have the honour to be, &c.,

James A. Gordon,
Captain of His Majesty's Ship *Seahorse*, and senior officer of His Majesty's Ships before Alexandria

To the Council of the town of Alexandria.'

Gordon later wrote to Lydia that he had given the town 'pretty hard terms', but they were well within the usages of war and, being neither cruel nor vindictive by nature, he permitted the Lieutenant who delivered them to the Council considerable latitude. For example, when the Council protested that it lacked the power either to recall goods sent out of the town after 19th August, or to compel citizens to assist in raising sunken vessels that were to be carried off as prizes, these points were accepted. When requested to define the term merchandise, the officer explained that it applied to exports such as tobacco, flour, cotton and bale goods. Finally, he was asked whether Gordon required the delivery of more merchandise than could be carried away, and replied that this was not the case. Once these points had been clarified the Council, having no alternative, submitted to the remaining terms.[10]

For the next three days the squadron concentrated on raising, rigging and caulking the sunken merchantmen and loading them. The streets were busy with seamen and scarlet-coated marines going about their business, but as the Clerk to the Council, Israel P. Thompson, subsequently reported to the committee set up to inquire into British activities in the Washington area, 'No private dwelling was visited in a rude or hostile manner, nor were citizens personally exposed to insult.'

The Washington debâcle cost Secretary of War John Armstrong and General Winder their jobs, but the Americans were recovering their balance very quickly. Commodore John Rodgers was summoned overland from Baltimore and, together with two more distinguished naval officers, Commodores David Porter and Oliver Perry, was given the task of trapping and destroying Gordon's squadron on its return passage down the Potomac. At their disposal were the crews of *Guerrière*, the recently restored *Java*, and *Constellation*, the latter blockaded in Norfolk harbour, plus those of Barney's men who remained after Bladensburg. Some militia elements, including artillery, were also present, but the task of punishing 'the base incendiaries' clearly belonged to the Navy. Indeed, the local press was quite specific on the subject: 'It is impossible that ships can pass such formidable batteries, commanded by our naval heroes and manned by our invincible seamen. We'll teach them how to draw up terms of capitulation!'

The first hint that Gordon might be in trouble came when Midshipman John Fraser of *Euryalus*, sent ashore to superintend some aspect of the terms, was ridden down by two mounted American naval officers. The bigger of the two grabbed him by the collar, hauled him across the pommel of his saddle and galloped off. Luckily for Fraser, the collar tore, enabling him to wriggle free and run towards the place where his boat was moored beneath a steep bank. The American pursued until he came face to face with the equally startled boat's crew, then rode away. Gordon mentioned the story to the amused editors of the Alexandria newspapers, who informed him that the two men were the captains of the warships that had been burned in the Washington Navy Yard and that Fraser's assailant had been none other than Commodore Porter.

Early on 1 September the 18-gun sloop *Fairy*, commanded by Captain H. Loraine-Baker, arrived with orders from Cochrane for the squadron to return to Chesapeake Bay. Loraine-Baker reported that he had had to fight his way past a 5-gun battery below Mount Vernon, and had observed several more batteries being constructed at various points along the river. The most difficult part of Gordon's mission had now begun, for if the squadron was trapped its loss would far outweigh the success of the entire Washington operation.

The squadron wasted no time in getting under way. With the exception of one ship which was unready and had to be burned, it was accompanied by the prizes taken at Alexandria, including three full-rigged ships, three brigs and bay and river craft, bringing the total number to twenty-one. In their holds were stowed 16,000 barrels of flour, 1,000 hogsheads of tobacco, 150 bales of cotton, and wine, sugar and sundry items to the value of $5,000.

The first part of the passage down-river was only slightly less difficult than it had been coming up, the wind being contrary and much warping being required. *Devastation* grounded and when it was seen that it would take some time to get her off, Rodgers attacked her after dark, using three fireships escorted by five armed boats. Captain Alexander launched his own boats, scattering the escort and diverting two of the fireships while *Seahorse*'s Midshipman John Moore courageously towed the third ashore.

Devastation was freed next day. Slowly, the convoy began trailing past Mount Vernon to drop anchor short of White House, on the Virginia side, where the Americans were constructing a strong battery on the shore. Their work was interrupted by *Meteor* with her bombs, joined by one of *Euryalus'* boats armed with a howitzer, and a captured gunboat, but since *Fairy* had passed some days earlier the number of guns in the battery had risen from five to eleven, and it was apparent that the Americans also had a furnace for heating shot. Gordon believed that it would be madness to attempt a passage without a fair wind and was prepared to wait for one.

On the 3rd *Aetna* came up to assist *Meteor* and was joined by *Erebus*, which had been engaged to little effect by three field guns during her passage. By the following day all the warships and prizes except *Devastation*, which was still five miles upstream, had reached the anchorage above White House. Gordon ordered the bomb vessels and *Erebus* to cease firing so as to conserve ammunition.

It must now have seemed to the Americans that the squadron regarded itself as trapped. Rodgers launched another fireship attack on *Devastation*, but *Fairy* was sent to her assistance and it was beaten off. Some of the attackers, possibly a party under a Lieutenant Newbold, hauled their boats ashore on the Maryland side and positioned themselves on a cliff from which they fired down into the ships, causing a number of casualties. The precise location is uncertain, although a British account describes it as being by or in 'a thickly wooded, narrow creek, protected by guns'. This party was in turn attacked by boats from *Devastation* and *Fairy*, and after twenty minutes' fighting was obliged to retire.

Next morning, 5 September, Gordon got the wind he wanted and briefed his captains. Covered by the high-angle fire of the bomb vessels, *Seahorse* and *Euryalus* slid downstream until they were within musket shot of the battery. 'The moment we brought our broadside to bear,' wrote Gordon, 'and anchored with the other frigate, to allow the prizes to pass under our cover, the enemy ran from their guns and opened a fire of musketry, but they were driven from their defences in an hour and a half.' The Americans, commanded by Porter, were hopelessly outgunned and were admired for their protracted stand, which cost them 29 killed and wounded.

At about 1500 hours, having silenced the battery, the two frigates cut their cables and followed the rest of the squadron, pushed along by a fine breeze. During the evening the ships came under long-range fire from two more batteries, located on a range of cliffs at Indian Head, on the Maryland side. These were under the overall command of Commodore Perry and, in Gordon's estimation, contained between 14 and 18 guns. At this critical moment, Gordon recalled: 'The *Erebus* grounded within range of the batteries, and the frigates and other vessels were called into action at once. The fire of the *Fairy* and the *Erebus* produced the most decisive effect, and the *Devastation*, *Aetna* and *Meteor* threw their shells with admirable precision.'

Since they had entered the Potomac three weeks earlier, Gordon's crews had known nothing but hard physical work, coupled with periodic action and the strain of constantly being behind enemy lines. None of them had enjoyed more than two full periods of unbroken sleep. In such circumstances the tempers of tired men fray very quickly. Aboard *Seahorse* the spark that came close to causing such an explosion was provided by *Euryalus*, which came gliding slowly past, masking her fire. Such was the fury of officers and gun crews alike that Gordon had to use the flat of his sword to prevent them firing over *Euryalus* at the American batteries. Black Charlie, having been publicly called to order by speaking trumpet, adopted a more suitable position.

By 2000 hours Perry's batteries had been silenced. The squadron dropped anchor for the night, *Erebus* was refloated, and next morning the convoy got under way again. By the evening of 6 September it had cleared Point Lookout, at the mouth of the Potomac, without encountering further opposition. Beating north up the Bay, it rejoined the fleet. Gordon had accomplished his mission at the incredibly low cost of seven killed and 35 wounded, and unexpectedly returned laden with booty.

Of his meeting with Admiral Cochrane, he wrote to Lydia: 'He had heard that the Americans were determined to oppose our passage and was on his way up the river, with all his ships and troops to assist us; he was very happy to see me and is much pleased with our exertions, and I am told he has particularly mentioned me to the Admiralty. He has given me the command of a squadron to cruise in the Gulf of Mexico and I sail in a few days for my command. I am happy the Admiral has ordered me southward for I was afraid of the winter. I do not expect to get more than £500 for our prizes, as Army and Navy share together. You will be astonished to hear that I never was in better health than now when I assure you that for three weeks I have had but little sleep, and the people had not their beds down for a month.'

His more formal report to Cochrane concluded: 'I cannot close this detail of operations, comprising a period of 23 days, without begging leave to call your attention to the singular exertions of those whom I had the honour to command, by which our success was effected. The many laborious duties which we had to perform were executed with a cheerfulness which I shall ever remember with pride. To Captain Napier I owe more obligations than I have words to express. It is difficult to distinguish amongst officers who had a greater share of duty than often falls to the lot of many, and which each performed with the greatest credit to his professional character. I cannot omit to recommend to your notice the meritorious conduct of Captains Alexander, Bartholomew, Baker, and Kenah, the latter of whom led us through many of the difficulties of naviga- tion, and particularly to Captain Roberts of the *Meteor*, who, besides undergoing the fatigues of the day, employed the night in coming the distance of ten miles to communicate and consult with me upon our further operations. So universally good was the conduct of all the officers, seamen and marines of the detachment, that I cannot particularise with justice to the rest; but I owe it to the long tried experience I have had of Henry King, the First Lieutenant of the *Seahorse* (to instance), that such was his eagerness that he even came out of his sick bed to command at his quarters whilst the ship was passing the batteries (the two first guns pointed by Lieutenant King disabled each a gun of the enemy); nor can I ever forget how materially the service is indebted to Mr Alexander Lothian, the Master, for finding and buoying the channel which no ship of a similar draught of water had ever passed with her guns and stores on board.'

In due course, as we shall see, Cochrane's dispatch would result in Gordon's receiving an appropriate reward. Forester, however, while providing details of the expedition in his *Naval War of 1812*, was clearly concerned lest his readers, and especially other authors, should establish the connection between Gordon's mission and Hornblower's parallel activities in *The Commodore*. In professional authorship terms this was perfectly understandable because he had no wish to upset his American readers and, moreover, a number of the books and stories in the Hornblower cycle had still to be written. He refers to Gordon by his surname alone, so creating a smoke-screen penetrable only by the most enthusiastic researcher; comments that the expedition 'met with more success than it deserved', so discouraging further investigation; and suggests that the time taken compromised the subsequent attack on Baltimore, although, as we have seen, the expedition actually drew off a considerable number of the city's defenders. This was quite uncharacteristic of Forester and one can only sympa- thise with his predicament.

American opinions on the subject are quite different. John Armstrong, the dismissed Secretary of War, can hardly have entertained much fondness for Gordon, yet he comments that his operations were conducted with 'a combina- tion of skill, diligence and good fortune'.[11] Again, it would, perhaps, be difficult to find a more patriotic, or fair-minded, American than Theodore Roosevelt, who in turn was Secretary of the Navy, led his Rough Riders in their epic charge up Kettle Hill during the Spanish–American War of 1898, and became President of

119

the United States.[12] Writing in his own *Naval War of 1812*, with which Forester must have been familiar, he says of Gordon's expedition, 'It was a most venturesome feat, reflecting great honor on the captains and crews engaged in it.'

NOTES

1. Later General Sir Charles Napier, best remembered for having conquered the Indian principality of Sind during a remarkable campaign in 1843.
2. At this period Commodore was not a rank but a temporary appointment conferred on the senior Captain of a squadron, lapsing as soon as he moved to other duties.
3. Parker launched an unsuccessful night attack on a militia camp near Waltham Farm, in the course of which he lost his life.
4. Brigadier-Generals William Winder and John Chandler commanded a 2,000-strong American force encamped at Stony Creek, near Hamilton, Ontario. Neither took adequate steps for the security of the camp, which was overrun by 700 British regulars under Brigadier- General John Vincent in a night attack on 6 June 1813. Winder and Chandler were captured together with all the American artillery and baggage.
5. Three steps trotting followed by three steps marching.
6. The Superintendent of Public Buildings estimated the cost of repairs as:

North wing of the Capitol	$457,388.36
South wing of the Capitol	$329,774.92
President's house	$334,334.00
Public offices	$93,613.82
TOTAL	$1,215,111.10

   The sandstone of the President's house was so badly stained by smoke that it was painted white and was henceforth known as 'The White House'.
7. A cousin of Lieutenant-Colonel Charles Napier's, mentioned above. As Admiral Sir Charles Napier he restored order to the eastern Mediterranean in 1840; forced the Egyptian army to evacuate Beirut; subsequently commanded the Allied Baltic Fleet during the Crimean War.
8. Hornblower's squadron in the Baltic consisted of one 74, two sloops, two bomb vessels and a cutter, and was therefore comparable to Gordon's in its firepower and abilities, although it lacked a rocket vessel.
9. It would have been strange if Forester had not set Commodore Hornblower a comparable navigational problem. The scene of this was the Frisches Haff (now the Zalew Wislany) in the Gulf of Danzig. By coincidence, the Frisches Haff resembled Chesapeake Bay in that it was landlocked save for an entrance at one end, although it was much smaller. That entrance was closed by a defended log boom except at its southern end where shallows denied passage to large vessels. Hornblower sent some of his boats through the shallows at night and these destroyed 35 coasters and barges within the bay. As the raiders' retreat was now cut off, they burned their boats and crossed the spit of land to the open sea, where Hornblower had more boats waiting to take them off.
10. Victory, as the saying goes, has many fathers, but defeat is an orphan. During the recriminations which followed the British operations in the Washington area, the unfortunate authorities of Alexandria were all but accused of collaborating with Gordon and were only able to prove the contrary with considerable difficulty.
11. John Armstrong, *Notices of the War of 1812*, vol. II, p.133.
12. An account of the attack on Kettle Hill can be found in the author's *Impossible Victories – Ten Unlikely Battlefield Successes*, Arms & Armour Press.

Chapter 10
THE STARS AND STRIPES

It is now necessary to go back a week or two to the time when Ross' troops were marching back to their transports from Washington. Inevitably there were stragglers, some of whom were merely footsore, but there were others who were intent on obtaining plunder, drink, food and female company to ease the hard lot of a soldier's life. They made a great nuisance of themselves and so outraged the inhabitants of Upper Marlborough that, at the urging of Dr William Beanes, a 65-year-old physician, it was decided to take action against them. On 26 August Beanes and former a Governor of Maryland, Robert Bowie, led a posse who apprehended six of the looters and clapped them in the Queen Anne gaol. A seventh man escaped.

Hurrying along the road to Nottingham, he came across the troop of mounted artillerymen who were now screening Ross' withdrawal. At 0100 hours on 27 August they galloped up to Dr Beanes' home to arrest him. He, together with two guests who were innocent of the foray, were put on farm horses and taken to the encampment at Benedict. Before they left the gunners warned the residents of Upper Marlborough that unless the stragglers were released by noon the town would be burned to the ground. They were set free immediately.

Bowie arrived at Benedict to plead for his neighbours but was also arrested. Somehow his politician's professional plausibility secured his release, but his farm was stripped of provisions. Dr Beanes' guests were also released when Ross received a petition from the citizens of Upper Marlborough confirming their innocence.

Dr Beanes, however, was in serious trouble. Of his part in the stragglers' arrest there was no doubt. Furthermore, he had been born in Scotland and in British eyes he had taken up arms against his lawful sovereign. That was treason, for which the punishment was death by hanging. Luckily for him, one of his neighbours was the brother-in-law of a successful Washington lawyer, Mr Francis Scott Key, who willingly undertook to plead for him.

Key first went to see President Madison, who had returned to Washington and had himself accredited as a government emissary to the British commander. Next he visited the British wounded, supplied them with writing materials, and offered to deliver their letters to the fleet, which he found lying off the mouth of the Potomac on 7 September.

Aboard *Tonnant* he met Ross and Cockburn. At first neither was inclined to be receptive to his arguments, but Ross, to Cockburn's disgust, changed his mind when he had read the British prisoners' letters, all of which confirmed that they were receiving excellent treatment. In such circumstances he felt that there was nothing to be gained by hanging an elderly general practitioner who had allowed anger to cloud his judgement. He therefore penned a note to Major General John Mason, the American officer responsible for prisoner exchange, to the effect that Beanes would be released, 'not from any opinion of his not being justifiably detained, nor from any favourable sentiment of his merit, but purely in proof of the obligation which I feel for the attention with which the wounded have been treated.'

By now, Gordon's squadron had rejoined and the entire fleet was heading up Chesapeake Bay to attack its next objective, Baltimore. Key was told that in the circumstances neither he nor Beanes would be permitted to land until after the attack, lest they disclose British plans; in the meantime they would be accommodated aboard the prisoner exchange ship *Minden*.

The direct approach to Baltimore lay up the River Patapsco, but access to the harbour itself was denied by a line of sunken blockships and Fort McHenry, which was a much stronger fortification than Fort Washington and further protected from close-range naval bombardment by shoal water. However, by landing at North Point, at the mouth of the Patapsco, the troops could reach Baltimore, sixteen miles distant, where they would find themselves confronted by strong entrenchments thrown up on the outskirts of the city. An alternative route lay up the Ferry branch of the river, although this was also covered by at least one battery and the approach march to Baltimore was longer and would involve a crossing of the upper reaches of the Patapsco. In overall command of the city's defences was Major General Samuel Smith, a local man, while commanding Fort McHenry was Colonel George Armistead, a professional artilleryman, both men of a very different stamp from the incompetent Winder and the drunken Dyson.

The plan of attack decided upon by Cochrane and Ross resulted in the troops landing at North Point early on 12 September. They marched steadily along the peninsula until, at its narrowest point, they found themselves opposed by some 3,200 militiamen at Gadfly Wood. Smith did not expect his men to stand for long, but before they broke, leaving behind 163 killed and wounded and some 200 captured, they inflicted 319 casualties on the landing force. One of them was Ross, shot dead by a sniper as the battle began. A popular and humane officer, his death brought tears to the eyes of many of his hardened veterans.

His successor, Colonel Arthur Brooke, continued the advance until he was in sight of Baltimore's defences, then camped for the night. Next day he examined the chain of redoubts and entrenchments which clearly had ample guns and fairly bristled with bayonets; in fact, about 13,000 militia had been concentrated in and around Baltimore and they would certainly fight well behind such works as these. The opinion which Brooke communicated to Cochrane was that his men would undoubtedly storm the works, but at prohibitive cost. Cochrane had already sent Black Charlie Napier up the Ferry branch with nine boats to create a diversion, and although this had succeeded in drawing off a considerable number of the defenders, he decided that the risks involved in a direct assault were not justified and sanctioned a withdrawal.

One chance of achieving another major success remained. Since 0500 hours on the 13th some of his ships had been bombarding Fort McHenry. If the fort surrendered the blockships could be blown up, and Baltimore could then be held to a far greater ransom than Gordon had extracted from Alexandria, no matter how many militiamen were present. Because of the shoal water only shallow draught vessels and the lighter frigates could be used in the bombardment, and even they could only engage at maximum range. In the bombardment line were most of Gordon's squadron, including *Meteor*, *Aetna* and *Devastation*, supplemented by two more bomb vessels, *Terror* and *Volcano*, the rocket ship *Erebus* and the frigates *Euryalus*, *Severn*, *Havannah* and *Hebrus*.

The bombardment continued throughout the day and on into the night. The frigate's balls, their force diminished by the distance they had travelled, smacked harmlessly into the thick masonry walls. Shells in their hundreds soared upwards from the bomb vessels, the course of their high-angle flight marked by smoke trails from burning fuses; some exploded inside the walls while others, their fuses too short, burst above them.[1] From time to time *Erebus* let fly a salvo of rockets. Altogether, some four hundred shells and rockets exploded within Fort McHenry, but because the casemates had been stoutly constructed, little serious damage and few casualties were caused. Likewise, though the American gunners stuck to their weapons, their return fire barely touched the warships.

This noisy and spectacular firework display was anxiously observed by non-participants on both sides. As *Seahorse* drew too much water to qualify for a place in the bombardment line, Gordon watched the effect of his ships' fire through his telescope. Farther out, Dr Beanes and Francis Scott Key were watching from the deck of the *Minden*. Distance and clouds of drifting powder smoke obstructed their view and Beanes, worried about the outcome, kept asking Key whether the American flag was still flying above the fort.[2] Key, who wrote poetry in his spare time, was scribbling lines on a piece of paper. With rising irritation, he replied repeatedly that it was. Beanes, glancing over his shoulder, read something about 'the rocket's red glare' and left the lawyer to his scribbling.

The bombardment did serve one useful purpose however. Covered by its noise and a rainstorm, Brooke's troops disengaged silently that night and marched back to North Point. At 0700 hours on the 14th the guns fell silent and by evening the last of the men were aboard their transports. Cochrane, depressed by his failure to capture Baltimore and by the loss of Ross, put the best face he could on the result in his dispatch by saying that 'the demonstration had been carried sufficiently far'. Gordon, writing to Lydia, commented that the decision to withdraw had been correct, adding that he had several wounded soldiers aboard.

Before the ships began dropping down the Bay, Dr Beanes and Francis Scott Key had been set ashore as promised. That night, amid the general celebration, Key completed his poem in a Baltimore tavern, setting it to a tune he had picked up aboard *Minden*. The tune was entitled 'Anacreon in Heaven' and had been composed by a John Stafford Smith specially for the Anacreontic Society of London, the major activity of which seems to have been drunken singing. Key's work was first published on 20 September in the *Baltimore Patriot* as 'The Bombardment of Fort McHenry', but it soon became known as The Star-Spangled Banner' and after a little while was regularly sung as the National Anthem of the United States of America. Curiously, Congress did not grant it official status until 3 March 1931.

Cochrane's fleet did not remain long in Chesapeake Bay. Leaving sufficient ships to maintain the blockade, it sailed for Jamaica where, having received further troop reinforcements, it prepared for a descent upon its next major objective, New Orleans.[3] Elsewhere, the blockade of the United States' eastern seaboard continued, together with a number of smaller combined operations. One such actually resulted in the surrender of a huge area of Maine east of the River Penobscot, including 100 miles of coastline and much of the territory separating New Brunswick from Lower Canada.

British and American peace commissioners had been meeting at Ghent for some time. News such as this, coupled with the Washington débâcle and the virtual bankruptcy of the Federal Treasury, placed the American commissioners at a serious disadvantage. The successful defence of Baltimore helped a little, but it was not a victory. On the other hand, the defeat of a British flotilla at the Battle of Lake Champlain on 11 September helped a great deal, since it denied the main invasion route from Canada to the British for the remainder of 1814 campaigning season at least. At last the commissioners had something with which to bargain. As their British counterparts were equally anxious to conclude the war, common sense prevailed. On Christmas Eve the Treaty of Ghent was signed, restoring the *status quo ante bellum*. In future, the Royal Navy would not impress American seamen because, with the defeat of France, it had no need to; and the Americans, rather than trying to conquer Canada, would expand westwards, which was the logical direction. It would, unfortunately, take weeks for the news of the Treaty to reach the New World, and until it did, fighting on land and sea would continue.[4]

New Orleans was an objective which had been chosen in London without due consideration of the difficulties involved. Situated on the Mississippi some eighty miles from the sea, it was an unsuitable target for an amphibious operation not only because the river approaches were covered by two strong forts, but also because much of the land on either side consisted of woods and almost impenetrable swamps. However, to some extent these difficulties could be overcome if the landing force, commanded by Major-General Sir Edward Pakenham, Wellington's brother-in-law, were transported in boats across Lake Borgne, after which it faced a comparatively short march before emerging on the Mississippi above the forts and some seven miles downstream from the city itself.

Although an American gunboat flotilla was easily defeated on the lake, the transportation difficulties had been seriously under-estimated. Having disembarked on 15 December, it took the leading brigade eight days to reach the river. On the night of 23/24 December the American commander at New Orleans, Major General Andrew Jackson, raided its camp, supported by two small warships, *Carolina* and *Louisiana*. When reinforcements arrived the attackers were beaten off, but the presence of the warships had not been suspected and no further advance upstream could be contemplated until they had been neutralised. Ships' guns were sent for, but these did not arrive until the 27th. *Carolina* was then set ablaze with red hot shot, but *Louisiana* escaped upriver. An attempt by British warships to force their way past Fort St Philip, 65 miles downstream, was unsuccessful.

Jackson had meanwhile begun constructing formidable earthworks on the left bank of the river, two miles from the British camp. Somewhat downstream and on the right bank were more earthworks capable of firing into the flank of any attack on the main position. Both sets of defences had one flank resting on the river and the other on impassable swamps, and so could only be assailed frontally. Jackson had about 5,000 men available, including a small contingent of regulars, Tennessee and Kentucky volunteers, some local militia and a number of pirates. Of these, some 3,000 held the entrenchments and the rest, considered to be unreliable, were kept in reserve.

Pakenham's plan involved sending one regiment across the river to capture the right bank defences while the main assault was delivered on the left bank. When the attack was launched on 8 January those detailed to attack on the right bank were delayed. Packenham, dangerously over-confident, ordered the assault to proceed regardless. The result was that his men were exposed to a murderous crossfire. He paid for his mistake with his life, but 2,100 of his soldiers were killed or wounded in attempts to storm the earthworks. Ironically, the attack on the right bank succeeded, but only after the main assault had failed. American losses amounted to seven killed and 70 wounded. After this the landing force withdrew and, wisely, Jackson did not attempt pursuit.

If there were joy in Washington at the result of the battle, this was tempered with sorrow a few days later when one of the Navy's big frigates, *President*, was run down and captured by a British squadron as she tried to break out of New York. On the high seas, further naval engagements took place on 20 February, when the USS *Constitution* captured the corvette *Cyanne* and the sloop *Levant* off Madeira, and on 23 March when USS *Hornet* captured the sloop *Penguin* off Tristan da Cunha.

Gordon was not directly involved in the Battle of New Orleans, for, as he commented to Lydia, 'the ground is too soft for my wooden leg'.' But as almost all the fleet's boats had to be used to transport and supply the landing force, he was inevitably involved in organising the considerable logistic effort required. He was evidently also involved in supplying arms and ammunition to the Creek Indians, who had allied themselves with Great Britain, as one of his letters mentions that he is going up the River Appalachicola in western Florida, which was one of their strongholds. During these operations he served under Rear-Admiral Pulteney Malcolm, who paid due tribute to his 'unwearied and cheerful assistance' in his dispatch. Gordon might well, as he had been promised, have been given command of a squadron in the Gulf of Mexico, had the war continued. Instead, to his immense pleasure and surprise, he received the following letter from the Admiralty, dated 3 January 1815.

'Sir – The Prince Regent, acting in the name and on the behalf of His Majesty, having been graciously pleased, in consideration of your eminent services, to confer on you the distinction of Knight Commander of the Most Honourable Military Order of the Bath, I have the commands of my Lords Commissioners of the Admiralty to acquaint you that you are to assume the style and dignity of Knight Commander of the said Order accordingly, in pursuance of the notification of the Royal Pleasure ...'

The honour had clearly been granted shortly after the arrival of Cochrane's dispatch on the Potomac operation. Given the time that the letter must have taken to reach him, and the fact that such matters were regularly published in the *London Gazette*, Lydia must have known that she had become Lady Gordon weeks before James was informed that he was now a knight. Sir James Alexander Gordon would spend the rest of his life in the Royal Navy, and although he had fought his last battle, the award made a very satisfactory conclusion to an active service career which he had begun as a wild, illiterate boy, and which spanned twenty-two years.

NOTES

1. At this point it seems appropriate to repeat Forester's comment in *The Hornblower Companion*: 'If Hornblower were not safely employed up the Baltic there was the danger (which I did not like to contemplate) that it would be his bombs that burst in the air over Baltimore!'
2. The flag was very large indeed, measuring 36 feet in the fly and 29 feet at the hoist.
3. Among them was Black Charlie's *Euryalus*, following a brief refit at Halifax. Bored by blockade duty, he challenged *Constellation*, which was still at Norfolk, to come out for a single-ship duel. The challenge was accepted and due arrangements were made in the most gentlemanly fashion. To everyone's annoyance, the war ended before the duel could take place.
4. It was this situation, it will be remembered, that provided the seed bed in which Forester's plot for *The Happy Return* began to germinate.

Chapter 11
HONOURS AND AWARDS,
CORONATIONS AND KINGS

G ordon brought *Seahorse* home to learn that Napoleon had escaped from Elba in March and that, once again, all Europe was on the march. The emergency ended with Wellington's decisive victory at Waterloo on 18 June 1815, following which the former Emperor was packed off to the remote island of St Helena with Admiral Sir George Cockburn for company on the voyage.

This, together with the end of the American war, meant that the Royal Navy's demobilisation plans were put into immediate effect. As they returned home, ships were paid off and de-commissioned, *Seahorse* among them. Of the 581 warships in commission at the time of Waterloo, only 368 remained three months later, more than 50 per cent of them still at sea. At the height of the Napoleonic Wars, the Navy's strength had reached a figure of 145,000 officers and men. This had already started to fall, but when the manpower requirements were reduced to 33,000 in 1816, and to 19,000 the following year, hardship for many, officers and men alike, was a foregone conclusion. The officers at least had their half pay to fall back on, but for the thousands of seamen, many of whom squandered their back pay and prize money in wild celebration on being discharged, the future was bleak. Even those with landsmen's trades were hard put to find work, for the combined effects of the Industrial and Agricultural Revolutions were already reducing the number of jobs available, and for these the seamen found themselves in keen competition with thousands of discharged soldiers. In such a fiercely competitive labour market, wages were low and conditions sometimes harsh. Small wonder, then, that the ports were thronged with near destitute seamen who would once have shunned the Service but now, if they were unable to obtain a berth in a merchant vessel, longed for its security.

Gordon, like Hornblower, was lucky to obtain a sea command, and in this his record gave him an enormous advantage, even if the prospects of future promotion now seemed very long term. On 7 November 1815 he took over *Madagascar*, one of the new generation of frigates, and commanded her in home waters for the next year. On 24 October 1816 he turned over to another frigate, *Maeander*. Some seven weeks later she was almost driven on to a lee shore in a heavy gale off Orfordness. According to the *Dictionary of National Biography*, 'for many hours she was in the greatest danger, and her ultimate safety was attributed mainly to Gordon's coolness, energy and skill'.

His reunion with Lydia had been a joyous occasion resulting in the birth of a son, also named James Alexander, on 19 March 1816.

His father had now retired to Gordon Hall, accompanied by Fanny, who maintained a regular correspondence with Lydia:

'We dined one day at Colonel Forbes' where we met a Colonel and Mrs David Forbes, who are lately married. She was a Miss Forbes from Essex. She was with a party at Southend when the *Madagascar* was at Sheerness, and went on board to see it, but you and James were on shore. Mrs F. spoke much of the attention of Dr Swayne, Mr Glascock, and the other officers. She met you and James at a ball given by the officers on board either the *Queen* or the *Northumberland* a few days after. She is very plain, but very genteel and ladylike in her manner. She had no idea that James was my brother, but she heard Isabella Forbes and I speak of Dr Swayne and she asked "if that gentleman was a surgeon in the Navy?" When I said he was, she mentioned how attentive and polite he had been and added, "It was on board the *Madagascar* frigate, commanded by a Sir James Gordon." "He is my brother," says I, but not before she had launched out in his praise, "being so much beloved by his officers and sailors". He is quite the fashion, and I never heard of any one so popular in a place as he is in Aberdeen with all ranks – it is astonishing, for he was very little there.'

Aberdeen was indeed proud of the part played by its more distinguished sons in the long war and on Wednesday 24 September 1817 the *Aberdeen Journal* contained a paragraph to the effect that 'The Magistrates and Council have conferred the Freedom of the City on Sir James A. Gordon, RN, KCB; Captain Arthur Farquhar, RN; Captain the Hon. William Gordon, RN; Sir Alex. Leith, yor of Freefield, KCB; Captain David Scott, RN; and Sir James MacGrigor, MD, Director General, Army Medical Department, in testimony of the esteem they entertain for them, and for the distinguished services they have rendered their country.'[1]

As Fanny describes to Lydia, Aberdeen was no longer the rather staid provincial town she and James had known when children:

'I did not look half dressed enough in the gay parties of Aberdeen, where satin, velvets or lace were the only things to be seen for elderly genteel women, and Kath's, though beautifully trimmed, looked nothing, for where you saw sarsnets on young people they were loaded with trim-mings, but lace and Chinese crape were the dandy. I really never saw such a height as dress has come to in Aberdeen. It makes one sick, I could not afford to live there (and visit) a month. Kath thinks it would be the height of bliss to spend the winter there, but she would be ruined before it was half over, if it were with nothing but chaise hire and hair-dressing. All the Grandees roll about in their carriages! When I used to be in Aberdeen years ago, a gentleman's carriage in the streets, shopping or paying visits, was never seen but at term time and the Meeting week, when the country gents came to Aberdeen; now they roll about the streets, the whole day and night, like London. I wonder they have not Hackney coaches, for the town is now so extensive that it really was a journey to pay visits in the forenoon – how tired I was of it. I was seldom off my feet from 11 o'clock till between 3 and 4. We would have had invi-tations for a month could we have stayed.'

In the spring of 1818 Gordon travelled to Aberdeen to receive the honour which had been bestowed upon him. Unfortunately no record of the ceremony appears to have survived. Since leaving Scotland as a boy he had spent very little time there and, as he had become almost a stranger to his own country, he used the occasion to make a tour of the Highlands with his father. In many respects life there had also altered beyond recognition. The power of the Clans was gone forever, swept away in the bloody aftermath of Culloden; now the Chiefs and a growing number of land owners had introduced the Cheviot sheep to their hills, producing far higher profits for them than the old cattle economy had ever done. To make way for the vast flocks, whole areas had been cleared of tenantry, many thousands of whom were forced to make a new life for themselves in the expanding industrial cities to the south or in Canada. Perversely, as the House of Stuart had long since ceased to pose a threat, Scotland as a whole and the High-lands in particular had become fashionable with the upper echelons of society. The very popular novels of Sir Walter Scott drew heavily for their themes on various aspects of Scottish history, influencing their readers to the extent that scenery, dress, language and customs regarded by Lowlanders and English alike as barbarous a generation earlier, were now seen as being romantic.[2] As always, something of a gap existed between perception and reality. The Gordons' journey took them from Aberdeen through Inverness to Fort William. As James's letter to Lydia indicates, much remains unchanged to the present day, but there were still numerous reminders, not only of the troubled past, but also that the average Highlander's life was terribly hard:

'We left Inverness at 7 o'clock, and went out by the very fine road, not inferior to any leading up to a nobleman's house in England, only not quite so broad. We soon came to the shore of Loch Ness, some parts of the road not six feet above the lake, and in others above 60, with the hill on our right hand, almost perpendicular, thinly covered with birch running up to 200 feet. The most dangerous part of the road is protected by a parapet, but even then, in some places, if one of the left wheels were come off, nothing could prevent the chaise falling into the lake. The road crosses many gullies on bridges. The Loch is quite large enough for a frigate to work to windward in; we could see nearly all the way up to Fort Augustus. We breakfasted at a beautiful place called Drumnadrochit. The lake here forms a deep bay and at the end of it a river runs into the lake. We stayed two hours and had a good deal of jaw with the landlord of the clean inn, who had been a servant of General Grant, Lord Seafield's brother, to whom the land belongs. The road goes round the bay, crossing the river half a mile above, where it falls into the lake. We looked down upon the old Castle of Urquhart, now in ruins. We stopped here, and the Laird went down to look at it, but it was too steep for me to venture.[3] We passed several little bits of ground under cultivation, but the fields are so steep they must be worked with the spade; then through a fine young larch wood, we looked quite down upon the family house of the Grants of Glenmorrison. A saw mill was put up there last year, but a flood quite ruined it; we were told the water was several feet above the bridge, and the trees that had been cut down were scattered about the banks; fortunately the bridge was not carried away. We passed the road to my friend, Mr Dick's property, but I heard it was 40 miles distant. On the south side of the lake we could see the vapour rising from the Fall of Foyers, and it must have been in great beauty just now. The first look we have of Fort Augustus is very fine. The hill we descended commands the fort, near the point where the Rebels placed their two three-pounders when they took the fort.[4] We landed at an inn, a King's house, not at all in repair, the landlord a very smart, clever little fellow. I went out to look at a steam engine that was at work.[5] The artillerymen touched their hats to me, and one of them came down, and we found him of great use to us when my father came down. We went to look at the canal, which in this part is not nearly finished. The

131

artilleryman took us all over the fort; there are only three soldiers and three officers.[6]

'We went to dinner and were much amused by our active little host. My father found out that one of the North Fencibles lived a little way out of the town and sent for him; the man was a great favourite of the Laird's, as I found out when Lady Betty made his appearance – Fanny will know him by the name. Lady Betty is a man as stout and tall as I am, and was dressed as a Highlander. We made him sit down with some whisky to drink while we took our wine. I was much pleased with the honest fellow, he has a great regard for the family – remembered me, asked if Fanny was going to be married, said he had seen Jane and Kate, was certain he should know Margaret, but did not know John or Charles, he asked for Mrs Gordon, and how many children I had, what I was going to do, and so on, without adding Miss or Mr to any name.[7] He then gave us an account of the losses the sheep farmers had this year; he has a small farm for which he pays £12 a year, which my father thinks is very much rent.[8] The Laird asked him for his family. He said he had put seven coffins from his house within as many months. One of his girls had married a soldier who had come to be paid off in England. They were acquainted before he went as a soldier, and were constant, and married on his return. Last month they went to settle in 'our America' [Canada], where his pension will be paid to him, which will enable them to take a good farm. "I tell you, Captain Gordon, next year I shall leave my land and go with all my family to that country; there is nothing to be done in this, here I shall starve; there I shall leave all my family comfortably settled when I die." When the poor fellow left, my father gave him 20s., but I had slipped as much into his hand at parting. I was astonished to hear from my father that the man who had been speaking so well, could neither read nor write.'

Lady Glenbervie died the same year. Following James's marriage to Lydia a certain coolness had crept into his relationship with his former patron, but Lord Glenbervie remained fond of his protégé and it was to him he turned in his hour of grief. It seems, however, that Lydia was neither inclined to forgive nor forget his early comments about her, for her daughters describe Glenbervie as being a 'poor, wayward, cynical, selfish old man', and as they were too young at the time to have formed such opinions for themselves, they can only have come from their mother. In fact, Lord Glenbervie was harmless enough, if a little tiresome at times, and he continued to perform the social round. When his duties permitted, James accompanied him to such fashionable centres as Bath.

'I went to the Pump Room with my uncle,' he wrote. 'I was pleased with the Ball, we were with Lady Duncan's party, she is a most pleasant woman. Several Captains were in uniform, but I was not at all sorry I was in a plain coat, for I was quite well known enough. I have had many interruptions in this letter. My uncle thought it quite right he should call on every lady he had spoken to at the ball, and for those who were not at home he left many kind messages. Yesterday we went at 9 to Sir George Shee's. We had music, harp, grand piano and fiddle played in a most masterly manner by one of the Miss Shees. The rest of the party went on to another, and I promised to remain until they came back at Sir George's, but I walked home as soon as they were off, and was snug in bed before they arrived. My uncle has a hundred places to take me this morning to call. He says he can never get through his calls. I don't think he can.'

In 1822 Lord Glenbervie died in James and Lydia's care.

If, perhaps, it is wondered why Lady Gordon was seldom present on these journeyings, the reason was that, at regular intervals, she was either adding to their family or nursing its newest member. Altogether, James and Lydia produced eleven children, of whom two died in infancy. Of those who survived, Hannah and James Alexander were joined by Lydia Christina in 1818; Maria Rosaro in 1820; Sophia Harriet in 1822 (died 1827); Salvadora Maxwell in 1823; Elizabeth Ann in 1825; Adelaide Louisa in 1827; and Sophia Margaret in 1830.

On 11 January 1819, to his great pleasure, Gordon was appointed to the command of his favourite ship, *Active*, then undergoing a refit. Captains no longer had to search for crews and a fortnight later he received the following letter from one of his old *Seahorse* hands:

'Sir – I wright these few lines to you hoping that you will take it into consideration for to send word to the Admiralty Office, so that I may optain my prize monney that's dew to me from the Seahorse frigate. I was Mr Pratt's servant on board the 2nd Class of Boys. Since I was paid off from the Seahorse I have mostly been stuard in merchants' vessels, and dewring the time I have learnt to play on the violine, and fife. Should such a person as that be wanted I would be happy to searve you Sir. No more att present.

I remain your most obegent and humble servant,
James Sarsfield.'

Whether the man was taken aboard is not recorded; the fact that his letter was preserved suggests that he probably was. He would certainly have been an asset on a dull voyage.

Active sailed for Halifax, Nova Scotia, in February 1819. Aboard was the new Bishop of Quebec, Dr Mountain, with his wife, son, two daughters, a Miss Stewart and a Captain Barrie, the last of whom incurred Gordon's wrath by losing his baggage on the way to the ship and thereby delaying her departure. Having delivered her passengers, *Active* re-crossed the Atlantic and spent some time in the Mediterranean. She was home again in the summer of 1821 and formed part of the squadron which assembled off Holyhead to escort the recently crowned George IV to Ireland.

'One of the finest days and sights I ever beheld in the bay fronting us,' wrote Lady Louisa Stuart. 'So presently we embarked in two boats, and, rowing round the (Royal) yacht, repaired to the *Active*, frigate, where we were most graciously received by Sir James Gordon. We were recalled to the pier in consequence of signals being made that the King was going to land, and took up our station in the balcony and topmost storey of the lighthouse. Captain Duncan and Sir James Gordon came up to us in the lighthouse."

Also present at Holyhead was that great society chatterbox and author of *Early Married Life*, Maria Josepha Stanley, who gushingly described Gordon as 'the exact model of an open-hearted, good-humoured, jolly English tar'. So sincerely meant was the compliment that not even a Scottish senior officer could possibly take offence!

The King's visit to Dublin, lasting from 12 August to 3 September, was a great success and some aspects of it were described by Gordon in his daily letters to Lydia:

'We are sorry the King could not have waited to come over with the squadron. We are told that when the King landed [at Dunleary] he made a speech to the people, which he ended by saying: "I shall leave it to your warm hearts to imagine what I feel on this happy occasion. I shall now bid you farewell, and I shall do by you as I know you will do by me – drink your healths in a good glass of whisky." No one knew H. M. was in the steamer until he got on shore and took his hat off to the people who had assembled ...

'I intended to have gone to Dublin with Duncan and Adam, but as I cannot walk as much as they would like, I have determined not to go up till the day of the Levée, and I shall not stay as I am poor and everything is now dear. A great number of people are constantly on board our ships, and I have left mine as I could not write there, and I am now on board the Royal Yacht and writing at the King's table. We hear that the Glasgow takes the body of the Queen over.[9] It is strange that Doyle (her Captain) was a midshipman in the ship which brought her to England ...

'I dined with Mr Ball. Mrs B is a sister of Admiral Whitshed; they have three daughters, something like the Admiral's but not such fine women – they have a great deal more to say for themselves as they are Irish. There was the finest illumination I ever saw in my life, not a window without lights, the town very quiet. This morning we went to see the review, and as I had never seen anything of the kind by King's troops, I was very well pleased, and as a lady was kind enough to allow me to get up on her carriage I saw much better. I met a great many officers I knew, and have several invites to dinner. Kiss our darlings for me ...

'After the review yesterday I went to put my name on the King's and Lord Lieutenant's books, and as Duncan and Adam got leave to dress in the room of one of the attendants, they asked Sir E. Nagle to allow me to dress in his room on Monday, so I shall have no difficulty in getting to the Levée ...

'I am afraid that the Drawing-room, which is to be held at night, will not pass without some young woman being squeezed to death. I am much pleased with the ladies, and we shall do our best to protect them from harm. There was a very large party at the Chief Baron's yesterday, no fewer than seven lords. The house is a noble one, and two very large rooms and a smaller one for refreshments were quite full. There was an illumination, and for fear the rooms should be too hot there were no candles put in the windows, and at last a stone was thrown which broke a pane, but on the windows being opened the mob was satisfied; only a few of the ladies were afraid.[10] We don't hear a word of the Queen, and whenever any of them proposes to cheer the King no one dissents; nothing can be more loyal. Today he goes to church in state, and I am told all the seats have been taken for months, and although it is not quite proper to mention the playhouse so immediately after the church, every box has been taken for seven months ...

'There was a most lovely young creature at the Chief Baron's, a Lady something de Burgh. I think she, with her mother and sister, want to go on board the *Active*, as Lady Clanricarde asked me to call, which I shall do.'

The following year, having now been at sea for almost 29 years, Gordon handed over command of *Active* and embarked upon a series of shore appointments which would enable him to spend more time with his growing family. Of these the appointment to the Superintendency of the Naval Hospital, Plymouth, in 1828, had the greatest bearing on his subsequent career. It was a task for which he was well equipped, for not only had his early years in the service taught him how the men of the lower deck thought and the sort of problems that troubled them, but his own good-humoured personality and massive presence enabled him to converse with them in a friendly, fair but firm manner, leaving them convinced that he would do his best for them. A number of his old hands would have been present to pass the word that one-legged Jem Gordon had been about a bit, seen more than his share of scrapping, had a vast experience of ships and men, and ate sea-lawyers for breakfast.

Young James entered the Navy on 16 March 1829, three days before his thirteenth birthday, passing the examination for Lieutenant on 6 May 1835. Doubtless to Lydia's relief, his early years in the service were not marked by battle and sudden death as those of his father had been. Indeed, apart from the bombardment of Algiers in 1816, which put an end to the activities of the Barbary corsairs, the destruction of a hostile Turkish fleet at the Battle of Navarino in 1827, and the capture of Spanish slavers in a number of single-ship actions, the post-war Royal Navy was under-employed.

When George IV was succeeded by William IV in 1830, Captain Sir James Gordon received an order to attend the latter's Coronation in Westminster Abbey. Naturally he wore full dress uniform but, to his great annoyance, was also ordered to wear the long crimson mantle of the Knights of the Bath. This, coupled with his height, made him a very prominent figure. When he left the Abbey after the ceremony he began to walk back to his hotel but at the corner of an alley he was jostled by a crowd of roughs, one of whom shouted, 'By God, that's Jem Gordon! He flogged me in the *Active* – now, mates, let's settle him!" Refusing to be intimidated, Gordon put his back against a wall and bellowed back, 'I don't remember you, but if I flogged you in the *Active*, you damned rascal, you deserved it!' The crowd, good humoured because of the occasion, cheered him and held back his assailants while he continued on his way.[11]

In 1832 he was appointed to the important post of Superintendent of Chatham Dockyard. The yard is no longer in commission but has been carefully preserved and much of it remains as it was in Gordon's day. The next few years, however, were to be the unhappiest of his life. On 23 December 1832 his father died at the age of 82. The event itself was not unexpected, but the two had always been close and, coming as it did only seven months after the death of Lydia's last baby, it was a sombre reminder of mortality. The title 'of Wardhouse and Kildrummy' went to James's elder half-brother John, now head of the Spanish branch of the family, as did Cookshill, Gorryhill and various other properties in Aberdeenshire.[12]

Hardly had these losses been absorbed than Lydia died on 28 July 1835 after a short illness. She and James had been married for 23 years and the attachment between them was as strong at the end as it had been at the beginning. Although he was still healthy and vigorous, clearly had an eye for a pretty face, and took as much pleasure in the company of women as they did in his, he never remarried. If, as time passed, there were liaisons, they were discreet and went unrecorded.

It took him many months to recover from his grief. His duties helped, his daughters were a comfort, and his family and friends were supportive, but the pain remained. He had his name placed on the books of the yacht *Chatham*, hoping that the familiar sights and sounds of the sea would dull its edge. Often he would stroll with the younger girls along the dockyard's anchor wharf, pausing to point out one of *Active*'s old anchors as though it were a priceless relic, then stand for a while staring at it in contemplation of happier times. In the end, of course, it was the children, his own and his numerous nieces and nephews, who brought him round. They had their games, their own small triumphs and tragedies, and they demanded that he share in them all. He still had his bad days but after a time he discovered that he could face the future again.

He was now at the top of the Captain's List. On 10 January 1837 he learned that he had been promoted to Rear-Admiral. As Dockyard Superintendent was a Captain's appointment he would have to leave Chatham – and the probability is that he was glad to do so.

NOTES

1. The same edition contained two further items of interest. One related to the death in Dumfries on 6 August of Mrs Janet Paul, aged 80, the only surviving sister of John Paul Jones, the Father of the United States Navy. The other dealt with the trial for burglary of John Davidson and James Henderson at Aberdeen. Davidson failed to appear and a sentence of fugitation was passed on him. Henderson pleaded guilty and received a sentence of transportation for fourteen years, 'after a very proper address from Lord Justice Clerk'.

2. Scott was given the task of stage-managing George IV's visit to Edinburgh. At one point the King appeared publicly in a fanciful version of Highland dress, looking a little odd.

3. 'The Laird' was James's nickname for his father.

4. His grandfather had been one of them, hence the emphasis. Having taken the fort, the rebels blew up some of its defences, using nineteen barrels of gunpowder. After Culloden, Cumberland's regiments used the fort as the hub of their operations in the Highlands. In a cistern among the ruins they found the bodies of several members of the original garrison, all of whom seemed to have been deliberately drowned. This can have done little to soften the troops' attitude to the Highlanders and serves as a reminder that in such wars atrocities were not the prerogative of one side alone.

5. Steam power was increasingly becoming a fact of life. In 1818 the SS *Savannah* became the first ship to cross the Atlantic with the aid of steam power, although she was primarily a sailing ship.

6. Fort Augustus had been repaired after the Forty Five but was now manned on a care and maintenance basis only. In due course it was decommissioned and was later modified for use as a school.

7. Nor would he. In the extended family of the Clan, the man would have regarded the Gordons almost as kin and feel quite comfortable in his informality.

8. Sheep farming in the Highlands had to be undertaken on a large scale if it were to succeed; a small-holder courted disaster if this were his only means of income.

9. The eccentric, and deeply unhappy, Queen Caroline, who had requested that she be buried in her native Germany. The King detested her and her death made no difference whatever to his plans for the visit to Ireland.

10. Before the age of mass media or a national press able to reproduce illustrations, crowds would gather at occasions such as this, just as they do today at show-business events, in the hope of catching a glimpse of the great, the good and the beautiful. It gave them an opportunity to shout comments, which were not always favourable, and this acted as something of a social safety valve. On this occasion the Dubliners did not like the windows being closed – or perhaps the curtains being drawn – but were happy enough once they could see what was going on inside.

11. Later in life, Adelaide Gordon told a slightly different version of the story in which her father was helped out of the crowd by some of his old sailors. The episode may have provided the germ for Forester's short story 'The Point and the Edge'. By coincidence, Hornblower served Commander-in-Chief Chatham between 1832 and 1835, and, had he existed, would have been in daily contact with Gordon. One night, he had dined out and the conversation revolved around whether the point or the edge of the sword produced the best results. Hornblower favoured the point and when he was attacked by a rough while walking back to the Dockyard, used the discussion to practical effect with his stick, disabling the man with a thrust to the throat. Gordon used a walking-stick at all times; why Hornblower needed one is uncertain.

12. John had joined his uncle James in Spain during his early years and become a wine merchant in Xeres, where he also acted as British Consul. He had married there and embraced the Roman Catholic faith. In 1834 he contributed £1000 of the £1,600 needed to erect a Catholic chapel at Huntly, presumably from his inheritance.

Chapter 12
THE GOVERNOR

On 6 July 1840 Rear-Admiral Sir James Alexander Gordon was appointed Lieutenant-Governor of the Royal Naval Hospital at Greenwich. This had been founded by Charles II as an institution for the relief and support of old and invalid sailors, 'who by reason of age, wounds and other disabilities shall be incapable of further service at sea and unable to maintain themselves'.

It consisted of a number of very fine buildings, including the Queen's House, designed by Inigo Jones, and the main range to which Wren, Vanbrugh, Hawksmoor and other distinguished architects contributed their talents during the century it took to complete. The establishment consisted of a Governor, a Lieutenant-Governor, five Captains, three Lieutenants, the Navy's Senior Physician, a Surgeon and six assistants, two Chaplains, a Matron and a staff of nurses aged under 45, many of them the wives or widows of In-Pensioners. In charge of each ward was a Boatswain.

The In-Pensioners received accommodation, keep, clothing, an allowance and medical attention. Not all of them were angels, nor, given the dangerous and violent life they had led, could they be expected to be. They were subject to Naval discipline and could be punished for bad behaviour, drunkenness and swearing. In extreme cases of misconduct an In-Pensioner could be expelled. Other punishments included confinement, living on bread and water for a period, temporary stoppage of allowance, restriction to the hospital grounds and even a compulsory badge for those unable to curb their language. There were times, as in every branch of the service, when officers could develop blind eyes and deaf ears, but everyone knew the limits.

The number of In-Pensioners at Greenwich reached its peak in 1814, when 2,710 were resident in the Hospital. Thereafter there was a slow but steady decrease resulting from the Navy's reduction to its peacetime strength and the granting of more Out-Pensions to men who could be looked after by relatives and friends. Nevertheless, when Gordon joined the Hospital the In-pensioners, in their smart blue, brass-buttoned coats and tricorne hats, were as common a sight in London as the scarlet-coated Chelsea Pensioners, and as highly respected by the public. They would be stood drinks and sometimes admitted free to places of entertainment; in return, they could be relied upon to oblige with a tale or two from long ago and far away.

Gordon's duties at Greenwich involved administration and welfare. After his earlier experience at Plymouth he settled into them easily. He enjoyed a good social life and became a well-known figure in several London clubs. He continued the custom, which he had begun with Lydia, of holding dinners on the anniversaries of the actions at Lissa and Pelagosa. To these he invited officers who had been present and happened to be in London. Of these days Mary Boyle, author of *Mary Boyle: Her Book*, published in 1901, retained some pleasant childhood memories. Gordon and Sir Watkin Pell, who, it will be recalled had also played a distinguished part in the action off Rota and was now the owner of a cork leg, used to dine regularly with her family. 'One day Sir James, on whose knee she was sitting, asked if she would like to see a race between two "one-legs". The dining-room was divided from the drawing-room by a long and spacious hall. This he proposed as their race course, and amid the clapping of hands large and small and cheering on, and the backing of Sir James Gordon (who was an idol) by the younger ones, the two admirals started, and Scotchman won in the canter to our infinite delight.'

The introduction of manufactured rubber made Gordon's daily life much easier, as by fitting a rubber cap to the base of his wooden leg the shock to the stump at each step was considerably reduced. Admiral Sir Harry Keppel, in his *Sailor's Life Under Four Reigns*, comments that he frequently used to walk all the way from Greenwich to London. Periodically Gordon also visited his property in Aberdeenshire, where Fanny lived until her death in 1843.

On 15 March 1842 Hannah, the Admiral's eldest daughter, married Mr John Charles Templer of the Inner Temple. They had six children of whom most were destined for the law, although their firstborn, James, entered the Army and in due course rose to the rank of Colonel, becoming superintendent of the balloon factory at Woolwich. The Gordons knew many people in mid-Victorian society and one of Hannah's younger friends was Thomas Hughes, the author of *Tom Brown's Schooldays*, who greatly admired her father.

The following year Maria followed the usual tradition of her mother's family by marrying a clergyman, the Revd. William Burnett, son of Sir William Burnett, a surgeon who had served aboard *Goliath* with Gordon at the Battle of St Vincent. They had four children, one of whom entered the Army and another married one of his Templer cousins.

Four years after these happy events Gordon sustained another tragic loss. The demands of the service had meant that the Admiral had seen comparatively little of his son. Since 1838 young James had served for a year in the *Niagara* (20) on the Great Lakes of Canada, then aboard Admiral Ommaney's flagship *Donegal* (78) off Lisbon. In August 1841 he was appointed First Lieutenant of the *Warspite* (50), serving on the North America and West Indies Stations, being promoted Commander on 15 October the following year. In January 1845 he obtained his first command, the sloop *Wolf* (18), and took her to the East Indies. While cruising off the coast of Borneo he contracted malaria and died on 6 January 1847. He was buried on the Island of Labuan. He had never married and one is left with the impression of a rather lonely figure; nor can it have been easy for him to follow so famous a father into the Navy.

During the same year two events took place which helped to soften the Admiral's private grief. First, the Governor, Sir Robert Stopford, died and was succeeded by Sir Charles Adam, an old friend of Gordon's. The two had not seen each other for some time and they worked very well together. Secondly, in June, Gordon was gazetted a member of the Navy's Medal Committee.

With the exception of the Waterloo Medal, issued in 1816, no campaign medals had been issued to either service for the French Revolutionary and Napoleonic Wars. Now, some thirty years after they had ended, the Government decided to issue Naval and Military General Service Medals to those who had survived and were still living. Each service would have its own medal with the engagements at which the wearer had been present listed on inscribed bars. The task of the respective service committees was to decide which engagements were to be listed and the basis upon which claimants' eligibility was to be judged. In this respect the generals had a much easier time of it than the admirals because the number of battles was already known, together with the identity of the regiments that had been present.

In addition to Gordon, the Naval Medal Committee consisted of Admirals Sir Thomas Martin, Sir Thomas Capell and Sir W. Hall George. The task facing them was Herculean as it involved, in some cases, casting the mind back over fifty years and considering the engagements fought by a total of 2,506 warships. At first it was proposed that Naval General Service Medals should be awarded only for those actions for which Gold Medals had previously been granted to flag officers and captains, but this was later extended to include not only all meritorious actions fought between 1793 and 1815, but also those which had taken place subsequently, up to 1840.

To simplify their task, the Committee sub-divided the bars to be issued into the categories of fleet actions, frigate and single ship actions, and boat actions. Needless to say the number of bars authorised was enormous.

The medals themselves became available for distribution on 25 January 1849. Unfortunately, death, emigration, illiteracy and a failure to advertise them properly all conspired to reduce the number actually issued to some 24,000 of which 21,000 had only a single bar. There were, for example, only 1,710 TRAFALGAR bars issued, 583 for 1st JUNE 1794, 351 for NILE 1798, nineteen for the action OFF ROTA, 124 for LISSA, 74 for PELAGOSA and 108 for THE POTOMAC; for some actions only one claimant came forward. Fourteen recipients carried five bars on their medals, and five had six bars. The maximum number of bars issued with one medal was seven (23 JUNE 1795; St VINCENT; NILE; OFF ROTA; LISSA; PELAGOSA and THE POTOMAC), the recipient being Rear-Admiral Sir James Alexander Gordon; KCB.[1] Inevitably the Committee's work was criticised on the grounds that some officers who were not present were listed as being associated with certain actions, while other actions which might justly have been included were entirely ignored. Given the immense scope of the Committee's brief, coupled with the unfavourable time lapse, some degree of error was unavoidable, but the fact was that honour had at last been done to many hundreds of gallant and deserving men. In fact the Committee seems to have applied some very strict conditions before it considered an action merited a bar. For example, that of the *Bordelais* with three French ships was one of those excluded from the list, although to lay eyes it seems as deserving as many. Had such a bar been issued it would have brought Gordon's total to eight. Its exclusion suggests scrupulous fairness on his part, and even those who raised their eyebrows when a Committee member was seen to lead the field by a wide margin could hardly deny that he had been present at all the engagements listed on his bars, and indeed played a leading role in four of them.[2]

In 1848 Gordon was promoted to Vice-Admiral. At about this time the Admiralty, anxious to maintain the numbers at Greenwich, announced that retired officers who qualified for admission to the Hospital could do so without forfeiting their half pay. Many, who lacked any other means of subsistence and lived in quietly in cheap rented accommodation, mainly in the West Country, were tempted by the prospect of rent-free apartments and other allowances. Sadly, for some the move was a bad one, as these advantages were more than balanced by the higher cost of living in London.

The Admiral was now well into his middle years and, though he could not fairly be described as stout, his figure had certainly filled to match his height. He must have weighed a great deal and this, as his daughters relate, contributed to the consequences of an unfortunate fall.

'It was in 1852, at a public dinner given to the Rajah of Sarawak, Sir James Brooke, with whom, through his son-in-law, Mr Templer, Sir James had become intimate, that he met with the accident which materially affected his health for the remainder of his life. Coming downstairs his wooden leg slipped upon some orange peel, and he fell with his right leg bent under his weight. He was quickly raised, got down the rest of the stairs, and drove home with Sir Charles Adam and a friend. He managed to get up to his own bedroom, when it was found that the tendons above the knee had been broken. Little could be done beyond reducing the swelling and inflammation, and giving perfect rest. He bore the inaction bravely and was cheered and entertained by the frequent visit of many friends, some of whom he had not seen for years. After some weeks he was carried downstairs to the library on the ground floor, where he had a small iron bedstead put up and where, in the daytime, he could be wheeled to the window which commanded a view of the river, which was a constant source of interest and amusement to him. But it was quite a year before he could use his leg even with crutches, and even then, his extreme nervousness impeded his moving about. Before this accident he had been accustomed to take a great deal of exercise in walking, which had conduced very much to his good health; this he never could do again, and no doubt he suffered in consequence. Through all these months, Sir Charles Adam never failed to come in and sit with him during the dark hours before dinner-time, when the two old friends were quite happy together.'

By the middle of 1853 Gordon had recovered sufficiently for him to succeed Sir Charles as Governor, an appointment which he retained for the rest of his life. On 15 January 1854 there came a further reminder of advancing years when his brother Charles died in distressing circumstances while returning from Greenwich to Scotland.[3] The two had always been close and in the autumn Gordon, now an Admiral, paid a visit to Scotland to help settle his affairs.

The Crimean War was now in progress. Although the Royal Navy played a smaller role in this than the Army, it was engaged in active operations in the Black Sea and the Baltic. Several of the Admiral's older friends, including Black Charlie Napier, were involved at the higher levels, and the Hospital received an intake of men too severely injured to continue their service. In 1855 the Admiral was honoured with the Grand Cross of his Order (GCB).

On 27 March 1856 his daughter Lydia, now aged 37, married the Revd. Edward Huntingford at Greenwich. Mr Huntingford was lively and forceful in his view of the Scriptures, to the point that his father-in-law, never a more than conventionally religious man, must surely have felt that his bonnet fairly buzzed with bees. He produced several books, including *Practical Interpretation of the Apocalypse* and *Popular Misapprehensions About the First Eleven Chapters of the Book of Genesis*; the latter evidently caused such uproar in clerical circles that it ran to a second edition.

Curiously, it was through Charles' eldest son, another Charles Edward, that the fighting blood of the Gordons, their wildness and originality, was passed on to succeeding generations. Born in 1816, he had purchased an ensign's commission for £2,000 in the 75th Regiment (later the 1st Battalion The Gordon Highlanders) in 1833. He served in the Kaffir Wars, and during the Indian Mutiny had commanded his regiment in a number of desperate actions, including the storming of Delhi and the campaign in Oudh, being commended for his 'coolness and judgement'.[4] The Admiral would almost certainly have got on well with him and been acquainted with the eldest of his thirteen children, several of whom made a name for themselves in various ways. Frances, born in 1852, he would have seen grow into a beauty like her great-grandmother, Katherine Douglas; happily, he could not have foreseen that she would acquire such notoriety that she would be obliged to live under an alias.[5] Stuart, born in 1859, he would have known as a boy; he had an active career in the Navy, the diplomatic service and the colonial police, but was less successful as a playwright.[6] Sylvester, born weeks after the Admiral's death, was, with others, granted a patent 'for improvements in the production of characters and lines on dials for clocks, watches, chronometers, and other graduated dials and scales, by photographic means'.

By 1860 the Hospital's declining numbers had convinced certain Admiralty departments that it had become an expensive white elephant. The Hospital Commissioners produced a deliberately negative report complaining about the In-Pensioners' leisure facilities. There was: 'A place of resort for smoking called Chalk Walk; a library not very liberally furnished and little frequented; some facilities for games of dominoes and draughts; these things, together with their meals and their beds, comprise nearly all attainable objects of interest.' If the library were little used, it was because many of the men remained illiterate; what they did enjoy most, however, was the chance to yarn with their mates over a pipe or two, and a game of dominoes or draughts, so it difficult to see what the Commissioners were complaining about.

If the Admiralty thought that closure of the Hospital could be brought about quickly it was mistaken. Its representatives were confronted by the towering presence of the Governor who made it clear that his In-Pensioners were there because they had satisfied the Board that there was no other place for them to live out their lives. For the moment, the Admiralty relented.

It was a last victory for Admiral Sir James Gordon and his old seamen, but inevitably a rearguard action. Together, they lived in an enclosed world of their own, strangers to the economic and social developments beyond the Hospital grounds. The country of their youth had changed almost beyond recognition; now there were factories everywhere, cities sprawling into the countryside, and railways winding through the land from one end to the other, and people spoke of different things. Even the Navy, where they might have felt most at home, had changed beyond belief. True, seamen still went aloft on gale-lashed nights to punch the wind, and would do for many years to come, but now steam ruled, the paddle-wheel had given way to the screw, warships were fitted with armour plate and powerful guns fired shells to unimaginable ranges. Those that could read followed the remarkable duel between the ironclads *Monitor* and *Merrimack* on 9 March 1862, and related it to those who could not, neither fully understanding what had taken place. They understood enough of change, however, to tell young sailors that they didn't know they were born, wistfully but with more than a little truth. What hurt them most was that, having themselves made history, they found they had little in common with the present.

By 1865 the number of In-Pensioners had dropped to 1,400. It was decided that there would be no more admissions, that the fitter men would be offered suitable Out-Pensions, and that the very aged and infirm could remain until their numbers declined sufficiently for the Hospital to be closed. In the meantime, Sir James Gordon would remain as Governor.

A Second Battle of Lissa was fought on 20 July 1866, this time between the Italian and Austrian Navies, ending in victory for the latter and, after several centuries of disuse, the temporary re-introduction of the ram. The Austrian commander was Rear-Admiral Wilhelm von Tegetthof, who had also distinguished himself two years earlier during Austria's and Prussia's war against Denmark and was only 38 years old. After Lissa, Tegetthof was sent to the United States to study naval developments during the recent Civil War. As his route took him through London, he made a point of visiting Greenwich to call on Gordon, the senior surviving British officer of the First Battle of Lissa. During their conversation Tegetthof courteously requested a photograph of the Governor, which was provided, and left one of himself, duly signed.

On 30 January 1868 Gordon was promoted Admiral of the Fleet. The once semi-literate boy had reached the pinnacle of his profession. By coincidence, he was concurrently the subject of a remarkable exchange of letters in *The Times*. When Sir John Burgoyne, with 70 years' service, was made a field marshal, a correspondent, signing himself 'Captain', pointed out on 9 January that Sir James Gordon's service spanned 75 years and was 'perhaps without parallel in either service'. This attracted a sour response from 'True Blue', who sounds suspiciously like one of those half-pay officers who had moved into Greenwich and was now, by force of circumstances, forced to move out again:[7]

'All honour to Sir James Gordon for the services he performed as a young captain more than half a century ago, and for which no officer in the Navy has been so handsomely rewarded. Sir James has never hoisted his flag or served afloat since he was advanced to flag rank, but has enjoyed the singular good fortune of doing hospital work with a comfortable house and income for more than a quarter of a century, and in consideration of his age and services in ending his days at Greenwich Hospital. The services of Field Marshal Sir John Burgoyne for his country have been of a more intellectual character and active nature at home and abroad as administrator, as warrior, as savant, than the hospital services claimed for Sir James Gordon.'

'Captain' retorted smartly on 13 January that it was quite misleading to describe Sir James's career as 'hospital services', and that he had been in action nine times. In fact, Gordon had been Gazetted nine times and as we know, in action many more than that.

The wards at Greenwich continued to empty and, as yet another New Year began, the Admiral complained that he was feeling out of sorts. He took to his bed and slept away what remained of his life. Where, one wonders, did his thoughts, hovering between sleeping and waking, take him during those last days? Did he once more lead the ships' boys of *Arrogant* in their rat hunts among the bilges, experience again the fearful sights and sounds of fleet actions, and smell the soft, spice-laden winds of the Caribbean? Or did he again command *Active* during her battles in the Adriatic, fight his way down the Potomac, or watch his bombs bursting over Baltimore's Fort McHenry? Perhaps his thoughts were gentler, returning to Lydia and his children, or the kindly, robust comradeship of the old seamen so long in his care, or the many friends who, year after year, brought him presents of walking- sticks and snuff boxes, more than he could possibly use in a lifetime. His life's work done, Admiral of the Fleet Sir James Alexander Gordon, GCB, died peacefully on 8 January 1869.

The Times marked his death with an Obituary of nineteen lines. Thomas Hughes thought this beggarly and the following month responded with an article entitled 'The Last of Nelson's Captains' in *Macmillan's Magazine*. In this he generously listed the Admiral's achievements, concluding with the comment: 'Heaven keep England from such a war as that in which James A. Gordon earned his Grand Cross of the Bath; but if England is ever fated to endure the like again, Heaven send us such captains as him and his peers.'

The Admiral was buried in the grounds of the Hospital, outside the old Nurses' Home, and his grave is marked by a simple tombstone. Apart from this, his portrait and a few papers, little remains to remind us of his long tenure of office at Greenwich. The Hospital was finally closed soon after his death, becoming the Royal Naval College in 1873. The Royal Hospital School, originally founded for naval orphans, continued to occupy the Queen's House and the flanking ranges to the east and west until 1933, when the school moved to Holbrook in Suffolk; in 1937 these same buildings were transformed into the National Maritime Museum.

The question remains, why did Gordon disappear so completely from view when the names of many of his contemporaries remain comparatively familiar? Part of the answer may be that Pellew (later Lord Exmouth), Black Charlie Napier and others all saw active service after the Great War of their times, and their names remained before the public; Gordon, on the other hand, as 'True Blue' spitefully pointed out, had not been in action since 1815. He would, of course, have been known throughout the Navy and he had a wide circle of friends, but the public gradually lost sight of him. The fact that his death all but coincided with the final closure of the Hospital may well have been another factor. The loss of his only son, too, meant that his direct line would cease. In 1890 his daughters Elizabeth, Adelaide and Sophia, concerned lest their father's services be entirely forgotten, gathered together his papers, correspondence and uncompleted autobiographical notes and published them under the title of *Letters and Records of Admiral Sir J. A. Gordon, GCB, 1782–1869*. Unfortunately, the sisters decided that the book, containing as it did so many personal letters, was for private circulation only among the Admiral's grandchildren, relations and surviving friends. Consequently few copies were printed, fewer reached library shelves and even fewer have survived. Sophia lived on well into the twentieth century, but Adelaide died in 1899 and Elizabeth the following year.

Fortunately, the Admiral's career had begun to attract the interest of the genealogist Mr J. M. Bulloch, MA, a Scot resident in London. Bulloch met the sisters and with their assistance he was able to pull together further aspects of the story that might otherwise have been lost. By 1906 he had collected sufficient material for a series of three weekly articles entitled 'A Famous Old Sailor – The Adventurous Story of Admiral Sir James Alexander Gordon, GCB', which appeared in the *Huntly Gazette*. These clearly aroused sufficient interest for him to be invited to address the Banffshire Field Club on 12 February 1909, the subject of his paper being 'The Gordons of Wardhouse and Beldorney'. The paper itself was long, scholarly, detailed and contained elements of dry and mischievous humour. Significantly, in his opening remarks Mr Bulloch commented that 'the family as we know it today is to all intents Spanish; and it has contracted a series of highly complicated intermarriages which have proved as difficult to grasp as the realisation of the proverbial "Castle in Spain".' Such a situation, followed by two more World Wars, provide further intelligible reasons as to why Gordon's career lay so deep in shadow for so long.

A quarter of a century later the *Margaret Johnson* docked and Forester set out to complete his research for *The Happy Return*. Already familiar with Gordon's career from his reading of the *Naval Chronicle*, he would have discovered his Letters and Records in the libraries of the British Museum or the Royal Naval College at Greenwich. Complementing the text, which itself fired the imagination, were a number of plates showing various actions, the Admiral at different stages of his career, and Lydia. With the professional writer's instinct for financial survival, Forester would have recognised that, if the public liked Horatio Hornblower, here lay an ample source for further plots; and that, lest others exploit the idea, it would be necessary further to conceal the already half-hidden entrance to the gold mine.

So it became part of Gordon's legacy that, while largely forgotten himself, he should contribute so much to the fictional Hornblower's life. Furthermore, Forester's hero was to inspire such authors as Alexander Kent, Patrick O'Brien and Dudley Pope to produce superb sea stories of the Napoleonic era. Deservedly, they sell in their thousands throughout the English-speaking world and beyond. It is thanks to Forester, and to them, that the world of James Alexander Gordon and his peers, with all its hardships, dangers and hard-won triumphs, remains vividly alive today.

NOTES

1. Gordon would also have been eligible for Davison's Nile Medal, personally awarded in 1798 by Nelson's prize agent to all officers and men present at the battle. As the award was private rather than official it does not appear to have been worn.
2. Hornblower 'died' in 1857 and would thus have received his Naval General Service Medal. It would certainly have included bars for ALGIERS and, had he been aboard, INDEFATIGABLE

20TH APRIL 1796. Of his fictional engagements, ROSAS would almost certainly have qualified, as would the capture of the Spanish frigate *Castilla* by the *Atropos* with *Nightingale*. The capture and sinking of *Natividad* by *Lydia* could well have been rejected by the Committee on the grounds that the first was an act committed – albeit unwittingly – against a friendly power, and the second because El Supremo was not a recognised belligerent. As to the rest, readers can award bars at their discretion, although the total is unlikely to equal Gordon's. On the other hand, Hornblower was awarded the *Légion d' honneur* for timely assistance provided for the future Emperor Napoleon III.

3. Colonel Gordon was travelling by train in a 3rd Class carriage. When, at Stafford, a drunk was pushed into his compartment, he rose to protest vigorously but was pushed back into his seat by the inspector. He was found to be dead on arrival at Crewe. A coroner's inquest decided that he had died from natural causes and, having been returned to Greenwich, the body was placed in the Hospital's mausoleum. However, three days later it was dispatched to Crewe for a second inquiry at which it was revealed that the Colonel was suffering from an acute heart condition. The body was then finally released for burial at Greenwich. At the second hearing a verdict of manslaughter was returned against the inspector. He was tried at Chester and, although acquitted of the charge, was dismissed by the railway company.

4. Lieutenant General Gordon was appointed Colonel of The Gordon Highlanders in 1895.

5. On 25 May 1881, aged 28, Frances married Lord James Torpichen, an officer in the Rifle Brigade, in Calcutta. Lord Torpichen left the Army the same year and the two returned home. Shortly after the birth of their fourth child in 1888 she attracted the attentions of a younger man, Lieutenant Lynche-Blosse of the York and Lancaster Regiment. An affair developed with the couple meeting in various places, including Llandudno, which no doubt seemed more discreet than Brighton. Llandudno, however, with its wide, curving promenade and geometric street plan, could have been designed with private inquiry agents in mind. The last straw seemed to be the setting up of a love nest at 97 Mortimer Street, Cavendish Square, London, where the lovers were known as 'Captain and Mrs Bailey'. Confronted with the evidence, Frances confessed to her husband, who promptly divorced her in a widely reported case.

6. His melodrama 'True Blue, or Afloat and Ashore' ran for six weeks at the Olympic Theatre, London, in 1893, but was adjudged a failure despite, as Mr Bulloch puts it with his usual deadpan humour, the attendance of the Duke and Duchess of Fife.

7. Despite the coincidence, 'True Blue' had no connection with Stuart Gordon, who was nine at the time!

Appendix
Ships' Histories

HMS *Goliath* (74) Third Rate

Built Deptford 1781; Displacement 1,604 tons; Complement 500

ARMAMENT: originally 24pdr guns on Gun and Upper Decks; two 24pdr guns plus ten 24pdr carronades on Quarterdeck; two 24pdr guns plus four 24pdr carronades on Forecastle; after being cut down and reduced to Fourth Rate in 1813: twenty-eight 32pdr guns on Main Deck; twenty-eight 42pdr carronades on Upper Deck, plus two 12pdr guns

1782 Captain Sir H. Parker: Barrington's Squadron, April; Kempenfelt's Squadron, May; Howe's Fleet, July; Relief of Gibraltar; 20 October encounter with Combined Fleet
1783–5 Guard Ship at Portsmouth
1786–9 Captain A. Dickson: Guard Ship at Portsmouth
1790 Captain Sir A. S. Douglas
1796 Captain Sir C. H. Knowles (from February)
1797–9 Captain T. Foley (from March): 14 February 1797 Battle of St Vincent; 1 August 1798 Battle of the Nile; Hood's Squadron, Alexandria; 25 August boats took ketch *La Torride*; 1799 Blockade of Malta; December paid off
1801 Captain W. Easington: June Commissioned; October Sailed for Jamaica
1802–5 Captain C. Brisbane (July 1802): 28 June 1803 took *Le Mignonne* (18) off west coast of San Domingo; August 1803 returned to England; 9 December boat attack on convoy off Sables d'Olonne
1805 Captain Robert Barton: 15 August with *Camille* (20) took *Faune* (16) in Channel; 16 August took *Torche* (18)
1806: Captain M. H. Scott (from December 1905): paid off
1807–8 Captain Peter Paget: February 1807 Commissioned; August Copenhagen Expedition; 1808 Baltic
1812 In ordinary at Portsmouth
1813 Reduced to Fourth Rate
1813–14 Captain F. L. Maitland: 1814 West Indies
1815 broken up

HMS *Racoon* Brig-Rigged Sloop

Built Deptford 1795; Displacement
317 tons; Complement 120

ARMAMENT: 14–18 guns/carronades

1795 Captain H. Raper: November
  Commissioned; Downs
1796 Captain Edward Roe (March):
  April took privateer *Le Furet*; 22
  May with others took privateer *Le
  Hazard* in Channel; 29 September
  took privateer cutter *L'Actif* (6) off
  Dungeness
1797–9 Captain R. Lloyd: 20 April
  1797 took privateer cutter *Les Amis*
  in North Sea; 11 January 1798
  took privateer *Le Policrate* (16) in
  Channel; 22 January took privateer
  La Pensée (2) in Channel; 20
  October sank privateer *La Vigilante*
  (14) in North Sea; 2 December
  1799 took privateer *Le Vrai Décide*
  (14) in Channel; 3 December took
  privateer *L'Intrépide* (16) in
  Channel
1800–3 Captain W. Rathbone (from
  December 1799): 1802 to Mediterranean; September Recommissioned and to Jamaica
1803 Captain A. Bissell; 7 June took
  schooners *La Vertu* and *L'Ami du
  Celonnot* (2) off Port au Prince; 11
  July took *Le Lodi* (20) in Leogane
  Roads; August took schooners *Deux
  Amis* and *Trois Frères* off Cuba;17
  August destroyed *La Mutine* (18);

14 October took gun brig *La Petite
  Fille*, schooner *Jeune Adèle* and
  cutter *L'Amélie*
1804 Captain James A. Gordon (from
  March): 2 April took privateer *Le
  Jean-Baptiste*; 5 April took privateer *L'Aventure* (1); 1 August took
  privateer *L'Alliance* (6)
Captain T. Whinyates
1805 Captain E. Crofton: 26 May took
  privateer *San Felix el Socoro* (2)
1806 April broken up

HMS *Mercury* (28) Sixth Rate

Built Thames 1779; Displacement
605 tons; Complement 163

ARMAMENT: twenty-four 32pdr
carronades on Upper Deck; two 6pdr
guns and four 18pdr carronades on
Quarterdeck; two 6pdr guns on Forecastle

1780–1 Captain Isaac Prescott: 6
  April 1780 sailed for Newfoundland; 1781 Johnson's squadron
1782 Captain W. Carlyon: to Hudson
  Bay
1783–6 Captain H. E. Stanhope
  (from September 1782): 27 June
  1783 sailed for Nova Scotia; July
  1786 paid off
1788–90 Captain A. Montgomery:
  May 1788 Commissioned; 12
  September 1788 sailed for Mediterranean

1796 Captain G. Byng: Newfoundland, and again in June 1798 and
June 1799
1797–1801 Captain T. Rogers (from
April 1797): 5 January 1798 took
privateer *Le Benjamin* (16); 15
January privateer *Les Trois Soeurs*
(16) ; 25 January privateer *La
Constance* (12), all on Lisbon
Station; 1799 Halifax; 5 February
1800 took privateer *L'Egyptienne*
(15) off Isle of Wight; Warren's
squadron off Cadiz; 5 May sailed
for Mediterranean;
20 January 1801 took *La Sans
Pareille* (20) in Mediterranean; 25
May 1801 attempt to recapture
Bulldog (18) at Ancona; 16
September with *Santa Dorotea* (36)
recaptured *Bulldog*
1803–5 Captain the Hon. D. P.
Bouverie: April 1803 floating
battery; 4 February 1805 took *La
Fuerte de Gibraltar* (4)
1805–7 Captain C. Pelly (from
August 1805): Newfoundland
1807–8 Captain James A. Gordon
(from June 1807): September
convoy to Newfoundland; 6 March
1808 sailed for Mediterranean; 4
April action with gunboats off Cadiz
1809 Captain the Hon. H. Duncan
(from November 1808): 1 April
gunboat *Leda* cut out from
Rovigho: 23 April with *Spartan* and
Amphion 23 April at Pesaro, 2 May
at Cesantico; 7 September schooner
Pugliese cut out from Barletta

1810 February–March paid off
Captain W. Webb: May commissioned
as troopship
1811 Captain J. Tancock (from
June): Lisbon
1812 Captain C. Milward
1813 Captain J. C. Richardson (from
May): Leeward Islands
1814 January broken up at Woolwich

HMS *Active* (38) Fifth Rate

Built Chatham 1799; Displacement
1,058 tons; Complement 315

ARMAMENT: twenty-eight 18pdr guns
on Upper Deck; eight 9pdr guns and
six 32pdr carronades on Quarterdeck;
two 9pdr guns and two 32pdr
carronades on Forecastle

1800–3 Captain C. S. Davers: 1800
convoy for East Indies; 26 January
1801 took privateer *Le Quirole* (14)
in Channel; 1801 convoy for
Mediterranean
1804–8 Captain Richard H. Moubray
(from August 1804): Blockade of
Toulon; 1804 took *La Jeune
Isabelle*; 1805 pursuit of Villeneuve
in Mediterranean; 1806 Irish
Station and Louis' squadron in
Levant; 19 February 1807 Dardanelles; 27 April took Letter of
Marque *Les Amis* (4); 26 March
1808 with *Standard* (64) took
Friedland (16) off Cape Blanco

1808–12 Captain James A. Gordon (from August 1808): 4 October 1809 sailed for Mediterranean; 13 March 1811 Battle of Lissa; 29 July boat attack on grain convoy near Ragomiza; 29 November with *Alceste* and *Unité* took *Pomone* (40) and stores ship *Persanne*; June 1812 paid off

1813–15 In ordinary at Woolwich

1815 Captain W. King

1815–17 Captain Philip Carteret (from October 1815): 1817 Jamaica

1819–21 Captain Sir James A. Gordon (from January 1819): Halifax

1822–3 Captain Andrew King (from December 1821): Particular Service

1825 Captain the Hon. Robert Rodney (from September 1824): Lisbon

1827 at Plymouth

1833 Receiving Ship; renamed *Argo*

1860 broken up at Plymouth

HMS *Seahorse* (38) Fifth Rate

Built Rotherhithe 1794; Displacement 984 tons; Complement 284

ARMAMENT: twenty-eight 18pdr guns on Upper Deck; eight 9pdr guns and four 32pdr carronades on Quarterdeck; two 9pdr guns and two 32pdr carronades on Forecastle

1794–5 Captain J. Peyton: Irish Station

1796–7 Captain G. Oakes: July 1796 with *Cerberus* took privateer *Calvados* (6) off coast of Ireland; 28 August with *Diana* and Cerberus took privateer *L'Indemnité*; 16 September took *Princesa* (16) off Corunna; 4 January 1797 sailed for Mediterranean

1797 Captain T. F. Fremantle (from July)

1797–1802 Captain E. J. Foote (from October 1797): 16 January 1798 with *Melampus* took privateer *La Belliqueuse* (18) off coast of Ireland; 8 March 1798 sailed for Mediterranean; 27 May took *La Sensible* (36) off Malta; August with Hood's squadron off Alexandria; 2 September with *Emerald* destroyed *L'Anémone* (6) at Damietta; June 1799 Naples

– surrender of French garrisons; October returned to England after grounding at Leghorn on 29 July; 23 May 1800 sailed for Mediterranean, Flagship of Admiral Sir R. Bickerton; 1801 Mediterranean; 1802 East Indies and home; October paid off

1803–5 Captain the Hon. Courtnay Boyle: 1803 Mediterranean; 11 July 1804 boats of *Seahorse*, *Narcissus* and *Maidstone* at Le Lavandou (Hyères); 4 May 1805 captured stores brig at San Pedro

1805–6 Captain Robert Corbet (from July 1805):1806 Jamaica

1806–11 Captain J. Stewart (from February 1806): 30 April 1807 sailed for Mediterranean; 5 July 1807 action with Turkish warships, *Badere-I-Zeffee* (52) (taken) and *Aliz Fezzan* (26) (sunk), off island of Chiliodromia; 8 May 1810 took privateer *La Stella di Napoleon* (2) June 1811 paid off

1813–15 Captain James A. Gordon: blockade duties off Cherbourg; 13 November 1813 sank privateer *La Subtile* (16) off Beachy Head; August 1814 Potomac operations; returned home and paid off

1819 July broken up

BIBLIOGRAPHY

Archibald, E. H. H. *The Fighting Ship in the Royal Navy 897–1984*. Bland-
    ford, Poole, 1984

Armstrong, John. *Notices of the War of 1812*. vol. 2, Wiley & Putnam,
    New York, 1840

Clowes, William Laird. *The Royal Navy – A History from the earliest times to
    1900*. vols. 4 and 5, Chatham Publishing, London, 1997

Davies, David. *Fighting Ships – Ships of the Line 1793–1815*.
    Constable, London, 1996

Forester, C. S. *The Naval War of 1812*. Michael Joseph, London, 1957

Goldsmith-Carter, George. *Sailing Ships and Sailing Craft*. Hamlyn, London,
    1969

Gordon, Elizabeth, Adelaide and Sophia, (eds.). *Letters and Records of
    Admiral of the Fleet Sir James Alexander Gordon, GCB*. Pubd. privately,
    London, 1890

Henderson, James. *Sloops and Brigs*. Adlard Coles, London, 1972

James, C. L. R. *The Black Jacobins – Toussaint L'Ouverture and the San
    Domingo Revolution*. Allison & Busby, London, 1994

James, William. *The Naval History of Great Britain*. vols. 3 and 5, London,
    1886

Joslin, E. C. *Spink's Catalogue of British and Associated Orders, Decorations
    and Medals*. Webb & Bower, Exeter, 1983

Lavery, Brian. *Nelson's Navy – The Ships, Men and Organisation
    1793–1815*. Conway Maritime Press, London, 1995

Lloyd, Alan. *The Scorching of Washington*. David & Charles, Newton
    Abbot

Lossing, Benson J. *The Pictorial Field-Book of the War of 1812*. Harper, New
    York, 1869

Lyon, David. *The Age of Nelson*. Ian Allan in association with The National
    Maritime Museum, London, 1996

Napier, Priscilla. *Black Charlie – A Life of Admiral Sir Charles Napier,
    KCB*. Michael Russell, 1995

Bibliography

O'Byrne, William R. *A Naval Biographical Dictionary*. John Murray, London, 1849

Parkinson, C. Northcote. *The Life and Times of Horatio Hornblower*. Michael Joseph, London, 1970

Price, Anthony. *The Eyes of the Fleet – A Popular History of Frigates and Frigate Captains 1793–1815*. Hutchinson, London, 1990

Roosevelt, Theodore. *The Naval War of 1812*. Scholarly Press, St Clair Shores, Michigan, 1970

Tully, Andrew. *When We Burned the White House*. Panther, London 1963

Warner, Oliver. *The Navy*. Penguin, London, 1968

The Aberdeen Journal, 24 September 1817

Dictionary of National Biography

The Huntly Express: 21 September, 28 September, 5 October 1906

London Gazette: 1803, p. 1229; 1808, p. 570; 1811, p. 997, pp. 893–4; 1812, pp. 450, 506; 1814, pp. 1940, 2080; 1815, p. 450.

Naval Chronicle: vol. 5, pp. 348–9; vol. 19, pp. 343–4; vol. 25, p. 430; vol. 27, pp. 260, 343; vol. 28, p. 263; vol. 31, pp. 353–7

Report of the Committee Appointed to Inquire into the Invasion of the City of Washington by The British Forces in August 1814. US Congress, Washington, 1814

Transactions of the Banffshire Field Club, 1908–9

INDEX